T0360933

Understanding Auctions

The book elaborates the basic principles of Auction Theory in a non-technical language so as to make them easily accessible to even those not trained in the discipline. Auctions as allocation mechanisms have been in use across the world since antiquity and are still employed in different countries for purchase and sales of a wide range of objects, both by governments and by private agents. Auction has gained popularity over other allocation mechanisms since the rules of auctions are very precise, involve much less subjective judgements compared to other alternative allocation mechanisms and lead to a more efficient process of discovering the true willingness of the buyers to pay. Moreover, the principles of Auction Theory are used in other contexts, for example in designing contests, or in controlling emission levels through allocation of permits and licenses.

Srobonti Chattopadhyay is Assistant Professor in the Department of Economics at Vidyasagar College for Women, Kolkata, India.

Rittwik Chatterjee is Assistant Professor in the Department of Economics at the Centre for Studies in Social Sciences Calcutta, Kolkata, India.

Routledge Focus on Management and Society

Series Editor: Anindya Sen

Professor of Economics, Indian Institute of Management Calcutta, Kolkata, West Bengal, India

The Focus series is designed to introduce management theorists and researchers (as well as the lay public) to a diverse set of topics relevant directly or peripherally to management in a concise format, without sacrificing basic rigour. The invisible hand of market has today been replaced by the visible hand of managerial capitalism. As the power and role of the managers have expanded, the world also has become more dynamic and volatile. To run their organisations more efficiently, the managers need to be aware of new developments taking place all around them. The Focus series addresses this need by presenting a number of short volumes that deal with important managerial issues in the Indian context. Volumes planned for the series will cover topics not only of perennial interest to managers but also emerging areas of interest like neuro-marketing. Some of the well established areas of research like bottom-of-the-pyramid marketing will be dealt with specifically in the Indian context, as well as critical developments in other fields, like Auction Theory.

Other books in this series

Poor Marketing
Insights from Marketing to the Poor
Ramendra Singh

Neuromarketing in India
Understanding the Indian Consumer
Tanusree Dutta and Manas Kumar Mandal

Understanding Auctions
Srobonti Chattopadhyay and Rittwik Chatterjee

For a full list of titles in this series, please visit: www.routledge.com/Routledge-Focus-on-Management-and-Society/book-series/RFMS

Understanding Auctions

**Srobonti Chattopadhyay
and Rittwik Chatterjee**

Routledge
Taylor & Francis Group

LONDON AND NEW YORK

First published 2020
by Routledge
2 Park Square, Milton Park, Abingdon, Oxon OX14 4RN

and by Routledge
711 Third Avenue, New York, NY 10017

Routledge is an imprint of the Taylor & Francis Group, an informa business

© 2020 Srobonti Chattopadhyay and Rittwik Chatterjee

British Library Cataloguing-in-Publication Data
A catalogue record for this book is available from the British Library

Library of Congress Cataloging-in-Publication Data
Names: Chattopadhyay, Srobonti, author. | Chatterjee, Rittwik, author.
Title: Understanding auctions / Srobonti Chattopadhyay and Rittwik
  Chatterjee.
Description: Abingdon, Oxon ; New York, NY : Routledge, 2020. |
  Series: Routledge focus on management and society
Identifiers: LCCN 2019016902 | ISBN 9781138575936 (hardback)
Subjects: LCSH: Auctions.
Classification: LCC HF5476 .C43 2020 | DDC 381/.17—dc23
LC record available at https://lccn.loc.gov/2019016902

ISBN: 978-1-138-57593-6 (hbk)
ISBN: 978-1-351-27108-0 (ebk)

Typeset in Times New Roman
by Apex CoVantage, LLC

Dedicated to our respected professor Krishnendu
Ghosh Dastidar, who introduced us to Auction Theory

Contents

x   *Contents*

Tables

Preface

The issue of allocation of resources in socially efficient manners remains central to the study of economics. How to best allocate a scarce resource still remains a debatable topic. However, auction as a method of allocation is acceptable to both the proponents of free markets as well as those in favour of command-and-control type economies. Auctions can take various forms and can be conducted equally well by government bodies and private entities. There are some inherent flexibilities in the structure of auctions that are unique to this allocation mechanism. This probably is one of the reasons why auctions have been in use since time immemorial. There are historically documented evidences of a multitude of types of auctions across the globe at different ages. Interestingly, auction has remained as popular as before, even in the present era. The most familiar of all auctions today include the auction of telecom spectrum licenses, auction of mining rights, auction of treasury bills etc. These are the auctions primarily conducted by governments. Private auctions at Sotheby's or Christie's are also quite well known worldwide. Besides these, there are a huge number of occurrences of auctions for allocating diverse types of objects. With the development of technology, electronic auctions have also been quite prominent of late. The auctions of different types of private possessions through e-Bay have been quite popular. With this growing popularity of auctions, many may find it interesting to have some basic information regarding the theoretical foundations of auction. There have been a few books, e.g., by Krishna (2010), Milgrom (2004), Klemperer (2004), Menezes and Monteiro (2008) and very recently by Ghosh Dastidar (2017). All these books, however, involve some technicalities that are not within the ready reach of those not trained in the discipline of economics. This book may therefore be regarded as a first attempt to make Auction Theory readily comprehensible to commoners. The theoretical aspects of Auction Theory have been explained in very simple ways, along with anecdotal evidences. Explaining intricate theoretical results in simple terms proved to be quite a challenging task. The efforts will be considered worthwhile if the readers find the reading of this book interesting.

Acknowledgements

The idea of this book is largely derived from the lecture notes used for the course Auctions: Theory and Practice taught at the Post Graduate Programme at Indian Institute of Management Calcutta in different academic terms during 2014–2017. The idea was first suggested by Anindya Sen, the editor of this focus series. His contribution, however, does not remain limited to this suggestion only; he has very patiently and meticulously gone through the chapters and offered valuable suggestions regarding their improvement. Thus it is primarily due to his support that this book came into being. The book concerns Auction Theory, a theory that both authors have learned from Krishnendu Ghosh Dastidar as his doctoral students, starting from scratch to various applications. In fact, Krishnendu Ghosh Dastidar's recently published *Oligopoly, Auctions and Market Quality* proved to be of great help in elaborating on the theoretical aspects of auction designs in various parts of this book. The elaborations on Indian auctions are to a large extent gathered from a working paper by one of the authors and Susmita Chatterjee. So we wish to take this opportunity to acknowledge her contribution in helping in the collection of information on Indian auctions. We wish to thank Soumyen Sikdar for his valuable comments and suggestions regarding the contents of the course Auctions: Theory and Practice, which subsequently proved quite helpful in designing the chapters of this book. We also wish to thank Anjan Mukherji, who has taught us how to explain theoretically complex issues in simple terms so that they are readily comprehensible even to those not from the discipline and Satish Jain for inspiring us to frame our thoughts logically. Finally, we wish to acknowledge the support that we have received from our respective family members, who largely helped us complete the book.

Abbreviations

BSE	Bombay Stock Exchange
BWA	Broadband Wireless Access
CBI	Central Bureau of Investigation
CCO	Coal Controller's Organization
CDMA	Code Division Multiple Access
CIL	Coal India Ltd.
CMPDIL	Central Mine Planning and Design Institute Limited
CMTS	Cable Modem Termination System
DHQ	District Headquarters
DoT	Department of Telecommunications
EAF	East African Flowers
EAS	Electronic Auction System
FCC	Federal Communications Commission
FCFS	First-Come-First-Served
GSM	Global System for Mobile Communications
HFCL	Himachal Futuristics Communications Limited
IPO	Initial Public Offering
MMDR	Mines and Minerals (Development and Regulation)
MOC	Ministry of Coal
MSTC	Metal Scrap Trade Corporation
NCDP	New Coal Distribution Policy
NDTL	Net Demand and Term Liabilities
NSE	National Stock Exchange
RBI	Reserve Bank of India
SDCA	Short Distance Charging Areas
SMR	Simultaneous Multiple-Round
TFA	Tele Flower Auction
TRAI	Telecom Regulatory Authority of India
UAS	Unified Access Service

1 What are auctions, and what is Auction Theory?

The word *auction* is more or less familiar to almost everyone in today's world. Very often daily newspapers carry reports on auctions of various types of public resources; at times there are advertisements, both from private concerns as well as from government bodies, calling for tenders for auction of some particular object(s) or the other. Advertisements or information about auctions are also common on websites. In many areas across the world, auction houses conduct auctions at fixed intervals of time, e.g., regularly on a weekly, fortnightly or monthly basis. We came across instances of auctions even in storybooks in our childhood.[1] Thus, almost everybody has a notion of what auctions mean. If asked, the first most likely answer to come from anyone selected at random is that auctions involve a situation where many people are trying to buy a particular object, and the seller of that object is asking for the price that each of the interested buyers is willing to pay; the buyers call out their prices, and in the process, the prices are driven upwards till the point where only one interested buyer remains. This is our most common perception about auction. However, this is just one form of auction, popularly known as *English Auction* and technically classified as open ascending auction.

So how do we actually define auctions? Auctions can be defined as market institutions with an explicit set of rules determining resource allocation and prices on the basis of bids from the market participants. The word *auction* is derived from the Latin word *augere*, which means augmenting.[2] In another opinion, the word *auction* originates from the Latin word *aucus*, which means increase.[3] Both these ideas point to the increasing trend in prices in the auctions. In most instances, auctions involve rising prices and therefore the name. But it must be noted that not all auctions follow this rule. Also, for most auctions, buyers are the bidders; however, even this rule has exceptions. For example, in the case of procurement auctions, the sellers are the ones who submit bids.

Although used widely in the present world, auction as an allocation mechanism has a rich history. We next provide a quick look at auctions in the historical perspective.

A historical perspective on auctions

Auctions as market institutions have existed since antiquity as a very useful allocation mechanism. As noted by Cassady (1967), a large variety of objects used to be sold through auctions in ancient times. Instances of auctions can be traced back to as early as 500 B.C.E. Herodotus mentions that marriage used to be conducted through auctions in Babylon during this era.[4]

In ancient Rome, auctions were used to a certain extent for commercial trade. The rules and modus operandi of these Roman auctions are not clearly known, but it seems that samples of goods were displayed in a particular place prior to their sale. However, whether the bidding process was of ascending or descending type or of any other type totally different from these is unknown. But the bids were likely to be of increasing type (meaning that the bids are higher for higher types of bidders and lower for bidders of lower types). Four types of agents were involved in these auction processes: one, on whose behalf the object was sold; another, who organised, regulated and possibly financed the auction sale; a third, who advertised, promoted the auctions and conducted the biddings; and finally the one who purchased the goods, being the highest bidder. The Roman Empire, it appears, used to host auctions of many other diverse types of objects. For example, during financial hardships, some people used to sell their furniture or ornaments through auction. It is said that in order to cover a deficit, some royal heirlooms and furniture were once offered for sale through auctions. The Roman soldiers also used to hold auctions in order to sell the proceeds of their loots during wars (sometimes even slaves were sold through auctions). This, it is believed, encouraged businessmen to accompany the military expeditions "in order to bid in the war booty at public auctions".

The strangest auction in history is probably the auction of the Roman Empire. The Praetorian Guard decided to sell off the whole of the Roman Empire through auction, after killing the Emperor Pertinax in 193 C.E. The highest bidder was promised that he would be awarded the crown. Didius Julianus, who agreed to pay 25,000 sesterces, or 6,250 drachmas per person, was the winner and therefore the emperor. However, he ruled for only two months and was beheaded by the insurgent groups headed by Septimius Severus, who then seized the capital. This is regarded as the earliest and most extreme case of "winner's curse".

Auctions were also used by Buddhist temples and monasteries in ancient China, as early as the seventh century C.E. The belongings of the deceased monks were offered for sale through auctions, and the proceeds were donated to the temples or monasteries. However, not much is known about the rules and methods of these auctions. Apparently, the auctioneer (usually a monk) had to know the normal price of the objects up for sale and had to provide details regarding the quality of these objects, e.g., whether old, new or worn out etc.

In England, auctions were also widely used. The historical accounts confirm that towards the end of the seventeenth century, sellers of pictures used to hold auctions in coffeehouses or taverns. Certain types of merchandise trade, the sale of properties of people who had gone bankrupt, the sale of estates and pieces of land etc. were also conducted through auctions. Whatever little information regarding the auctions in England in the old days is available suggests that the rules of auction were somewhat similar to those used at present. Sotheby's, the world-famous auctioneer company, was established in 1744, and another no less renowned auctioneer company, Christie's, was founded in 1766.

Auctions, like many other ideas and institutions, traveled to America with the emigrants from England. The colonisers, during their early days in America, used auctions for disposing of properties under the judicial process, to close out stocks of merchandise, to liquidate capital goods and inventories, to unload unsalable goods in the importer's possession at the end of the season, to sell second-hand furnishings, utensils, domestic animals etc. Before the American Civil War, even slave trade was largely conducted through auctions in the Old South.

In countries like the Netherlands, Germany, Japan, Hong Kong etc., auctions came to be used much later. During the second half of the nineteenth century, the auctioning of fish and produce developed in Germany and the Netherlands, respectively. In countries like Japan and Hong Kong, auction became a predominant mode of transaction, mostly as a part of the market reform that aimed at replacing the existing feudalistic structure in which the producers or primary sellers were largely exploited by the ruling authority.

In addition to fish auctions, the Netherlands has also been known for the Dutch flower auctions. Since the end of the nineteenth century, flower products in the Netherlands used to be marketed through the Dutch Auction mechanism. The flower growers during that time used to form a cooperative and developed their own local marketplace. The Netherlands remains the world's leading producer and distributor of cut flowers:

The Dutch dominated the world export market for cut flowers in 1996 with a 59 per cent share and for potted plants with a 48 per cent share. The world's two biggest flower auctions are in Aalsmeer (VBA) and Naaldwijk/ Bleiswijk (BVH); every day on average 30 million flowers – originating not only from the Netherlands but also from countries such as Israel, Kenya and Zimbabwe – are traded in 100,000 transactions. The Dutch flower auctions play a vital role in Holland's leadership of this industry, by providing efficient centers for price discovery and transactions of flowers between buyers and sellers. These auctions traditionally use the "Dutch auction" as the mechanism for price discovery. They are established as cooperatives by the Dutch growers. The following auction rules characterize the Dutch flower auction concept, see also Van Heck et al. (1997). Dutch flower auctions use a clock for price discovery, as follows. The computerized auction clock in the room provides the buyers with information on producer, product, unit of currency, quality, and minimum purchase quantity. The flowers are transported through the auction room, and are shown to the buyers. The clock hand starts at a high price determined by the auctioneer, and drops until a buyer stops the clock by pushing a button. The auctioneer asks the buyer by intercom, how many units of the lot he or she will buy. The buyer provides the number of units. The clock is then reset, and the process begins for the left-over flowers, sometimes introducing a new minimum purchase quantity, until all units of the lot are sold. In the traditional way buyers must be present in the auction room. In practice, it turns out that the Dutch flower auction is an extremely efficient auction mechanism: it can handle a transaction every four seconds.[5]

A very different type of auction has been discussed by Sen and Swamy (2004), which they term taxation by auction. This basically refers to a practice that was in use during the end of the nineteenth and early twentieth centuries in Gujarat, India. The state of Gujarat, located in the western part of India, has for quite some time been a major centre of manufacturing and trading. The producers/traders involved in any common line of business in a city in this region used to form associations known as Gujarati guilds. As Sen and Swamy (2004, p. 134) observe:

Like any professional association, the guilds sought to raise funds from their members for internal use, such as organizing dinners for guild members. In addition, the richer guilds collected funds to provide various community-wide public goods and services. . . . To raise funds, many Guilds employed a mechanism that the Gazetteer of the city of Surat, a prominent Gujarati trading and manufacturing center described as follows (Bombay Presidency 1877, p. 321): "A favorite device for raising money is for the men of craft or trade to agree, on a certain day, to shut all their shops but one. The right to keep open this one shop is then put up to auction, and the amount bid is credited to the guild fund."

Sen and Swamy (2004) theoretically analyse this mechanism and conclude that, under certain conditions, not only was this taxation by auction mechanism preferred by a majority of guild members over the conventional taxation mechanism, but also this mechanism ensures more equity socially compared to conventional taxation.

Thus auctions have been in practice for quite some time in different parts of the globe and in different forms for addressing a vast majority of issues and selling varied types of objects. They have evolved over time and are still evolving. Auction as an allocation mechanism is increasingly being adopted for the allocation of natural resources, especially scarce ones, across countries. The most remarkable examples are those of telecom spectrum licenses, licenses for mining rights, Treasury bills etc. Many new auction rules are still being devised to address the needs of contemporary times. With the development of technology, the ways of conducting auctions are also transforming. This is quite visible even in some traditional auctions. For example, in September 1994, through a referendum, the flower growers in the Dutch flower industry, who are also owners of the auctions, decided to ban foreign grower participation to reduce foreign access to the traditional Dutch Auctions. This in turn prompted the development and introduction of Tele Flower Auction (TFA) as one of the initiatives in response to import restrictions by the traditional Dutch flower auctions.

> *TFA is an electronic alternative that enables buyers to trade at a distance; this alternative is currently exploited by an import organization called East African Flowers (EAF).[6] Van Heck et al. (1997) show that: IT enables new ways of competition and coordination, thus changing the ways in which individuals and organizations exchange goods and services. It also shows the globalization of the flower market, and the increasing cross-border competition.*

Different types of auctions

Auctions can be of different types depending on their rules. The classification of auctions can be done in many different ways, e.g., open bid vs. sealed bid auctions, single stage vs. multistage or sequential auctions, private value vs. common value auctions etc. Within these categories, further subcategories exist. Also, some auction rule share some aspects of each category.

As the name suggests, open bid auctions are auctions for which the bidders call out their bids publicly, so that everyone present gets to know these bids while the auction is still going on. Sealed bid auctions, on the other hand, are auctions in which the bidders submit their bids in sealed envelopes. Here, only the auctioneers get to observe the submitted bids before declaring the winner. Usually the auctioneers have discretion to disclose, partly disclose or totally suppress information about submitted bids. For single object auctions, bid disclosure policy does not make any difference in the bidding behaviour. However, for multiple object auctions, the extent to which information about previous rounds is disclosed results in totally different bid functions in subsequent rounds.

Open bid auctions can be of the ascending or descending type. The auctions where the prices are driven up gradually are termed ascending price auctions or simply ascending auctions. As noted earlier, what is popularly known as English Auction is an open ascending auction. These auctions may involve a single object or a multitude of objects. Thus we may have single object English Auction or multi-object English Auction, depending on how many objects are up for sale. In case of a *single object English Auction*, the auction starts either by inviting bids from the bidders directly or by the auctioneer quoting a low price and asking how many bidders are willing to pay that bid. In the former case, bids are invited from the bidders continuously, and in the process the bid values keep on increasing, some bidders dropping out at several points, till the bid value reaches a level where only one bidder remains who is willing to buy the object at the quoted bid. This bidder is declared to be the winning bidder. In the latter case, the auctioneer keeps enhancing the bid value by a predetermined increment amount and continues to do so till all bidders except one drop out. The *multi-object English Auction* is similar in principle except for the single difference that that here more than one object are up for sale. Here also the prices keep rising, and the auction ends when the number of remaining bidders equals the number of objects offered for sale.

The auctions in which prices start from a high level and are revised downwards step by step are termed descending price auctions or simply descending auctions. Such auctions are popularly known as *Dutch Auctions*. This auction can also be for a single object or multiple objects. For single object auctions, the auctioneer begins by calling out a very high bid and asks whether any bidder is willing to pay. If no one shows interest, then the bid is revised downwards, and again it is asked whether any bidder is interested to obtain the object at the said price. If again nobody reflects any interest, the price is revised further downwards, and the bidders are asked again. The process continues till one bidder expresses willingness to pay the particular specified price. This bidder is identified as the winner. The object is then sold at the said price to this winning bidder. For multiple objects, the auction proceeds in the same manner, except that multiple prices are quoted from the beginning, and all those prices are revised downwards until all the objects are handed over to some interested bidder(s) at the specified prices.

Sealed bid auctions can also be classified into several categories. Just like open auctions, sealed auctions can be for single or multiple objects. For single objects, the most commonly practiced auction formats are first price and second price auctions. In the case of both these auctions, the bidders submit sealed bids, and the highest bidder is chosen as the winning bidder. In a first price auction, winning bidders have to pay their own bid, and in a second price auction, winning bidders pay the second highest bid. Theoretically speaking, many payment rules can be devised as combination of these two; for example, some payment rule may specify that the winning bidder has to pay a weighted average of highest and second highest bids where the weights add up to one.[7]

For multiple objects, auctions can be conducted in a single stage or in multiple stages. Multiple stage auctions are also alternatively called sequential auctions. In the category of single stage auctions, the most standard formats are Discriminatory Auctions, Uniform Price Auctions and Vickrey Auctions depending on the payment rules. In all these auctions, the bids are collected for all the units up for sale, then they are ranked vis-à-vis one another. The highest bids among these, equal in number as the objects, are selected to be winning bids. The same bidder may win all the objects, or the winners may be different. The maximum number of winning bidders, however, cannot exceed the number of objects offered for sale. In cases where there are predefined rules such that an individual bidder can obtain a maximum of one object or where the bidders have demand for just a single unit, the number of winning bidders exactly matches the number of objects.

In a *Discriminatory Auction*, subject to payment of these quoted bids, the objects are handed over to the bidder(s). Usually it so happens that different bids are associated with different objects and that therefore the winning bidders have to pay different prices for different objects (even when the objects are homogeneous units of the same commodity); this type of auction is termed a Discriminatory Auction. It is also alternatively termed a *pay-your-bid auction*. In the case of *Uniform Price Auction*, the same price is applicable for all the objects. This uniform price can be the highest losing bid, or the lowest winning bid, or any price in between. But in practice the general convention is to set the highest losing bid as the uniform price to be paid for all the objects. For example, suppose two objects are up for sale and there are three bidders. The submitted bid vectors are

$$b^1 = (10,4)$$
$$b^2 = (8,6)$$
$$b^3 = (5,2)$$

The two highest bids are $\left(b_1^1, b_1^2\right) = (10,8)$. So bidder 1 is awarded one unit, and bidder 2 is awarded one unit. Both the bidders will pay their bids, i.e., bidder 1 will pay 10, and bidder 2 will pay 8 in the case of Discriminatory Auction.

Considering the same example for a Uniform Price Auction, the highest losing bid is 6. So for this auction, bidder 1 is awarded one unit, and bidder 2 is awarded one unit. However, both of them will now pay 6.

The rules for a *Vickrey Auction* were suggested by the eminent auction theorist William Vickrey, and thus this auction is named after him. This auction is not generally used in practice, but the rules provide interesting insights for understanding many other issues related to designing auctions. According to the rules of the Vickrey Auction, every winning bidder has to pay as many highest competing bids (leaving out his or her own quoted bids) as the number of objects won. Again considering the same example, bidder 1 is awarded one unit, and bidder 2 is awarded one unit. However, here bidder 1 will pay 6, and bidder 2 will pay 5.

For *sequential auctions*, usually one object is offered for sale at each stage, and the auction continues till all the objects are sold off. The auction in each stage thus is a single object auction that can be conducted either in first or second price formats. If the first price auction format is used in each stage, then the sequential auction is a first price sequential auction. Similarly, if the second price auction format is used in each stage, then the sequential auction is a second price sequential auction. However, in some cases the first price auction format is followed in some stages and, in other stages, second price sealed bid auction. Such auctions fall in the category of hybrid auctions. In some hybrid auctions, even open auctions may be used in some stages.

In real life, depending on the contexts, several other auction formats are designed that are at times hybrid auctions, designed by combining two or more commonly known auctions as just discussed. At times some new auction rules, somewhat similar to a popular auction rule, are also devised. More detailed discussion on various auction formats, including the ones briefly just discussed, has been provided in a later chapter.

Auction Theory

Auction Theory is a systematic analytical study of auctions. Analysing and understanding auctions are done through the application of Game Theory, while designing auctions comes under the domain of Mechanism Design Theory. To elaborate on Auction Theory, therefore, it will be better to first discuss a little bit both Game Theory and Mechanism Design Theory, the two main pillars of Auction Theory.[8]

Game Theory is the study of multi-agent interdependent interaction. The term *interdependent interaction* means a number of persons or groups (whom we formally call agents) interacting with one another, with the utility of each agent partially dependent on the actions chosen by other agents, along with his/her own chosen action. In the standard context of rational utility maximising agents, every agent will always choose actions in order to maximise his/her utility (or expected utility as the case may be) keeping in mind the possible choice of actions by the other interacting agents. Thus, the description of a game must specify which agents are involved, and in the context of Game Theory, we term them *players*. It must also specify what actions the players may possibly choose; how the players are allowed to choose actions (i.e., simultaneously or one after another, and if so, then in which order the players choose actions etc.), which is formally termed *rules of the game*; and finally, the utilities (or expected utilities) of all players resulting from different combination of actions, formally termed *payoffs*. If any one of these components is unspecified, the description of the game is incomplete, and no solution for the game can be worked out. For a properly specified game, using the information provided, equilibrium outcome(s) can be worked out logically step by step, and thus the behaviour of the *players*, i.e., what actions each player will choose, can be predicted. Therefore, in Game Theory, the job is to predict what equilibrium outcome(s) will result under any specified information about games.

Mechanism Design Theory can be described as a reverse engineering of Game Theory. Here the players, the actions that can possibly be chosen by players and the utility to each player following the different action combinations are specified. The mechanism designer has some particular objective(s) in mind. The rules of the game have to be appropriately designed so that the players, always choose actions in their own interest such that the resulting equilibrium outcome fulfills the objective of the mechanism designer. Thus, basically the job is to find out the appropriate rules, following which the players will interact in such a manner that the mechanism designer's intended objective is attained automatically without any coercive methods.

Auction Theory is rooted in both these theoretical strands. Auctions can be modelled as games of incomplete information. This is how the equilibrium outcome that will result from an auction can be somewhat apprehended, though the actual outcomes may in some cases vary from the calculated outcomes due to lack of information about bidders in real life. Designing auctions is an application of Mechanism Design Theory, since to fulfill the auctioneer's objective, which may be ensuring efficient allocation or maximising expected revenue etc., the bidders need to be induced to act in certain desired ways. To ensure the fulfillment of the auctioneer's objectives, the rules of auctions should be so devised that the bidders have incentive to behave as desired by the auctioneer.

We need to mention here that Auction Theory is not limited to just studying auctions per se. It has wide-ranging applications in analysing and addressing many other problems related to resource allocation issues, designing contests etc. The scope and applicability of Auction Theory have been elaborated in the rest of this book.

Notes

1 In the famous book, *Ha Ja Ba Ra La*, by Sukumar Ray (1921), translated in English by Jayinee Basu as *HJBRL: A Nonsense Story*, we find reference of an ascending auction, where some of the characters suddenly get involved in bidding regarding a particular number. In many popular ghost stories also we find instances where some objects that had previously belonged to someone who is no more and that had been purchased through auction by somebody else evokes the deceased souls, leading to unnatural incidents in the vicinity of the objects.
2 Krishna (2010).
3 Cassady (1967).
4 Cassady (1967).
5 Van Heck (1997, p. 358).
6 van Heck, van Damme, Kleijnen, and Ribbers (1997).
7 When the highest and second highest bids are β_1 and β_2, respectively, the winning bidder may be asked to pay $a\beta_1 + (1 - a)\beta_2$.
8 For a detailed theoretical discussion on Auction Theory, Game Theory and Mechanism Design Theory, interested readers may look up Chapter 1 in Dastidar (2017).

2   Why study Auction Theory?

Introduction

Auction is an allocation mechanism that has been in use by both private and public enterprises since antiquity. As noted in Chapter 1, a multitude of objects can be and have been allocated by auction throughout the world. Auctions have been a common practice for many private enterprises. Private auctions can be conducted both informally and formally. In fact, there are no fixed features of private auctions. Such auctions can be conducted any time at any place for any object. At times there are certain designated markets where the transactions are always conducted by auction and no other mechanism. Some examples of this are the fish auction market in the state of Kerala in India, the flower auction markets in the Netherlands etc. However, auctions are sometimes used even in those markets where fixed price sales are the general norm. In these markets, auctions are used to sell off the stocks of unsold items slightly before the closing hours of the markets. This is particularly observable in markets where perishable goods are traded and there are inadequate storage facilities. One good example is that of vegetable markets where crates of certain vegetables (usually the ones more prone to perish quickly) are auctioned during the closing hours.

For private auctions, at times specific organisations are designated with the responsibility of conducting auctions, two ready examples of which being Christie's and Sotheby's. These are the two most commonly known auction houses that operate in more than one country. Both these auction houses have rich histories. Sotheby's was originally founded in London in 1744, while Christie's, also founded in London, came into being in 1766. Sotheby's is now headquartered in New York, while Christie's head office is still located in London. Both of them, however, have offices and salerooms in different parts of Europe, America and Asia. They also have representatives working on their behalf in several parts of the globe. Other than these big ones, there are many auction houses in various countries that operate locally and on smaller scales. The auctions conducted in these auction houses are generally more formal in nature compared to the auctions taking place in decentralised markets.

In the case of private auctions, the object being sold can often be sold using some other alternative procedure like bargaining. However, people at times prefer auctions over bargaining as the former process takes less time. Also, some people find the process of bargaining psychologically taxing, which is not the case with auctions.

Private auctions are guided primarily by individual objectives. Public auctions, however, are meant to be guided by social considerations. It is believed that scarce natural resources should always be allocated in a socially efficient manner for their best utilisation.[1] Efficient allocation is all the more important in the context of publicly owned resources. There are various alternative mechanisms for allocation of such resources. Some standard ones are First-Come-First-Served, Comparative Hearing, Beauty Contests, Lottery etc. Many countries have been using these mechanisms for various resource allocations for many years. But over time there has been a trend to shift to auction over these mechanisms. To identify the reasons for such a shift, it is important to understand the mechanisms in terms of their potential to fulfill certain desired objectives first and then assess their relative performances compared to auction.

First-Come-First-Served basis

The very term *First-Come-First-Served* (FCFS) suggests the process of allocation. The candidate who is the first to report obtains the object. When there is more than one object, then candidates who report earlier than others for as long as the objects are available for allocation obtain the objects. The prices are pre-specified unless it is a free allocation. Radio broadcasting licenses were allocated through this process in some European countries. The primary merit of this process is that it involves much less time compared to alternative allocation mechanisms. However, efficiency in allocation cannot be guaranteed in this process. The ones who are reporting early may not be the most efficient candidates, and there is no way to ascertain beforehand that the most efficient ones would report at the earliest hours. This process can result in socially efficient allocation only when the aspirants are more or less similar to one another so that it does not really matter which one gets the license, and therefore the licenses do not land up in totally inefficient hands. However, in reality this is a rare possibility. So to ensure socially optimal allocations, FCFS cannot be really regarded as a reliable option, particularly when the allocation relates to the granting of long-term rights.

Comparative Hearing

Comparative Hearing is very commonly practiced in the allocation of resources like spectrum licenses. For example, the Federal Communications Commission (FCC) in the United States, used to distribute spectrum licenses using this method for a long time. The idea behind using Comparative Hearing has been that the government or some agency authorised by the government must dictate how a public resource is to be used in order to ensure the socially optimal usage of the concerned public resource, i.e., the usage that confers the maximum possible benefit on the public. However, once the criteria for judging the best possible usage are understood, the aspiring candidates always project themselves accordingly so that, by ensuring high scores for themselves, they eventually ensure the allocation in their favour. In the absence of adequate scope for verification of the claims the candidates make, it is not possible to identify the most suitable candidate, and in reality in most cases the scope for verification of claims does not exist. Thus Comparative Hearing, though having more scope than FCFS to ensure a socially efficient outcome, may not always yield the intended result.

Administrative process

The Administrative Process of allocation is also popularly known as *Beauty Contest*. This has been one of the earliest processes of allocating spectrum licenses in Canada and the European Union.[2] The government or any government-designated authority lays down the basic criteria for allocation, and proposals are collected from the aspirants. Then an in-house committee consisting of experts is set up. This committee examines the proposals in light of the government-specified criteria. The advantage of this procedure is that the government has enough scope to fix selection criteria in line with broader plans or policies. Also, this procedure has some inherent flexibility for which the criteria can be updated as per requirements from time to time. However, an obvious shortcoming of this process is the amount of time involved in the selection. Moreover, a lot of subjective criteria are involved in this process, for which no objective rules can be set, e.g., the ability to implement the proposal, the feasibility of the proposal etc. Another important factor is that the selection committee enjoys a lot of discretionary power in this procedure; why some proposal did not get selected over the others is quite often not explained with adequate clarity or transparency. This leaves a lot of room for favouritism, which is quite likely to lead to inefficient allocation.

Lottery

Lottery as opposed to Comparative Hearing or Administrative Process of selection leaves little scope for any misuse of discretionary powers and at the same time involves much less time. This is also a much simpler process compared to Comparative Hearing or Administrative Process and is much less costlier as well. However, the first problem about this process to be noted is that, by its very nature, this process cannot guarantee an efficient allocation. The selection process being totally random, it can never be ascertained that the selected candidate is indeed the best one. This problem is all the more intensified when there exist huge disparities in the efficiency levels of the potential candidates (if the candidates are more or less similar to one another in terms of their abilities or efficiencies, then this problem is somewhat mitigated). However, there is no guarantee that the applicants are more or less equally efficient. In fact, as observed in the case of allocation of cellular licenses in the United States during the 1980s, the Lottery system attracted many speculative applicants who were not technically competent; they applied for licenses only to sell them later at very high prices, the net effect of which was a substantial loss of revenue for the government.[3]

Auctions

Auctions have over the years gained more popularity than the processes just discussed, and the reason for this is manifold. First of all, like Administrative Process, even auction as a procedure has a lot of inherent flexibility so that it can always be designed in line with government's broader objectives. But it has no scope for the subjective selection of candidates. If efficiency is the prime objective, then auctions fulfill it in the best possible manner as opposed to any other alternative allocation mechanism. An appropriate designing of auction can ensure that the best candidate among the applicants will end up being self-selected. This allocation process also helps in true price discovery. If the *highest bidder wins* principle applies, then along with ensuring efficiency, auction can also generate the highest possible expected revenue.[4] Auctions are less time-consuming compared to Administrative Process or Comparative Hearing. Auction has significant transparency in the allocation process. Thus auctions are growingly becoming more acceptable as an allocation mechanism worldwide, and their application is on the rise for a large variety of objects.

Application of principles of auctions in other areas

The principles of auctions can be used to understand certain other economic phenomena. The ready applications are in context of contests, lobbying and rent-seeking games. Across the globe, contests in various spheres are gaining more and more popularity. The contest organisers always aim at ensuring that the contestants put in their best efforts. The designing of the contest rules plays a key role here. Similarly, the behaviour of agents in the context of lobbying and rent seeking can also be understood in light of Auction Theory. How Auction Theory helps the understanding of these issues can be better understood once the theoretical formulations are discussed. Chapter 3 lays the theoretical foundation of auctions. Hence the theoretical analogy between auctions and contests, rent-seeking, or lobbying, is discussed in detail at the end of Chapter 3.

Notes

1 *Best utilisation* in this context implies the utilisation that maximises social welfare.
2 Jilani (2015).
3 Jilani (2015).
4 It is more or less reasonable to assume that the most efficient among the bidders will submit the highest bid and thus the revenue generated in the process will be the highest when the highest bidder is chosen as the winning bidder.

3 The economics behind auctions

Introduction

In this chapter, we look at the way auctions are modelled and analysed by economists. While we try to avoid technicalities, it is important for the reader to be able to appreciate the approach to building a general theory of auctions. We hope that the chapter will not contain anything that a slow and careful reading of the chapter cannot elucidate.

For any auction to take place, at least two types of agents must be present, the seller(s) and the buyer(s). At times some other types of agents may also be involved. On behalf of the bidders, there may be representative bidders, while on behalf of the sellers, there may be auctioneer(s).[1] The sellers are the group of people having objects for sale, while another group of people, who want to buy the objects from the seller(s), constitute the buyers. Depending on who are the bidders, i.e., the sellers or the buyers, the auction can be of two types. When the buyers constitute the bidders, we refer to the process simply as auctions, while when the sellers constitute the bidders, we refer to the process as procurement auctions.[2] One defining characteristic of auction is the presence of asymmetric information about the objects to be auctioned.

In every type of auction, for each of the objects both buyers and sellers have valuations. If the bidders are the buyers, then the valuation of an object for a bidder is the maximum amount of money he wants to pay for the object. For example, if a rare painting is being auctioned, a bidder may value it at Rs. 1 crore and therefore, Rs. 1 crore will be the maximum amount that the concerned bidder will be willing to pay for the painting. On the other hand, if they are the sellers, then the valuation of an object for a bidder is the minimum amount of money she wants to get for the object. The seller of the painting may not be prepared to sell it for any amount less than Rs. 50 lakhs. Note that the objects may be either multiple units of the same object or different items, which may be related or disconnected. If one object is to be sold through an auction, we call it a *single object auction* (also known as *single unit auction*); otherwise, we call it a *multiple object auction* (also known as *multiple unit auction*).[3]

The valuation of a bidder depends on the amount of information that the bidder possesses about the object(s) up for sale. This valuation may or may not be affected by observing the behaviour of other bidders and thus receiving more information about the object(s). When the valuations are unaffected by additional information revealed from the bidding behaviour of contending bidders, we are in a framework of independent valuation. On the other hand, when a bidder revises his valuation for any object(s), even once, by observing the bidding behaviour of others, we are in an interdependent valuation framework. However, in both these frameworks, one thing is common. Every individual bidder inherently possesses certain exclusive information that cannot be exactly observed by others, neither their contenders nor the sellers/auctioneers. Others will have only some probabilistic notion about it. The information that is inherently possessed by individual bidders is basically a signal. What differentiates these two alternative frameworks is the fact that in an independent valuation framework, the signal and the valuation are the same, while in an interdependent valuation framework, the valuation is some function of the signal.

The information that is exclusively possessed by an individual bidder is thus private information, which may be the actual valuation or the signal, depending on which valuation framework we are in. This private information (valuation/signal) of a bidder constitutes the *type* of a bidder. In auctions, the bidders with higher types (i.e., the bidders who have higher valuations for the object[s] up for sale) tend to bid higher, and a *positive monotonic* relationship can be observed between types and bid values; thus bidders of higher types will have higher bid values. Therefore, observing the bid values the types can be directly inferred. However, prior to the auctions, these bid values can be assessed only on the basis of expectations. Depending on the objective of the auctioneer and the calculated expected bid values, that auction format is chosen that fulfills the objective in the best possible way. If more than one auction format fulfill the objective equally well, then the auctioneer is indifferent between them. How well an objective will be fulfilled hinges on how accurately the bid values can be predicted beforehand. Due to the monotonic relationship between bid values and types, the exercise of calculating bid values boils down to calculation of the types in the most accurate way possible.

The underlying process of discovering the types of bidders is nothing but an application of Game Theory. Theoretical analysis of auctions is essentially a study of incomplete information games, where the bidders and the auctioneer/seller(s) (or buyer[s] for a procurement auction) are the players. Just like any other incomplete information game, at least one type of player possesses some private information; e.g., as mentioned, the bidders have private information about signals. If the bidders and the auctioneer(s), both have private information, and then the auction is a double auction.[4] For understanding the theoretical aspect of auctions clearly, it will prove helpful to first discuss what are incomplete information games. The following section is thus dedicated to outlining the basic idea of incomplete information games.

Incomplete information games

To discuss games of incomplete information, first let us define what exactly is meant by the term *game*. "A *game* is a formal representation of a situation in which a number of individuals interact in a setting of *strategic interdependence*".[5] Strategic interdependence implies that the welfare of an individual depends on not only her own actions but also on the actions of the other individuals. For example, if a person has a strong preference for a quiet environment, it is not sufficient that the person herself remains quiet; it is also important that the surrounding environment is free of noise. So a person who has a strong preference for a quiet environment will have a lot of disutility when the surroundings become noisy. Usually the utilities (or expected utilities) of the players are considered to be the indicators of their welfare. One essential underlying assumption in Game Theory is that of the *rationality* of players. By rationality, we mean that every player always chooses actions optimally given the level of information available to the player concerned. For example, suppose a person is due to meet a friend after a long time, and somehow he has forgotten to specify exactly where to meet, though they have agreed on a particular area of the city. If they are unable to reach each other's mobile phones, both will try to guess on the basis of the information they have about each other's preferences: what is the most likely place where both of them can find each other? Suppose person A knows that person B is fond of books, so person A will first look for person B in the bookshops in their agreed-upon area. If A knows that B was fond of one or two particular bookshops, then A will first visit those bookshops. B will also guess the line of action of A and thus actually wait for A in one of his favourite book shops. In such a situation, they will locate each other quite easily. However, if B has had a change of preference that A is not aware of, e.g., B prefers to be in a coffee shop rather than a bookshop, and B is also not conscious of A's ignorance about the changed state, then B will wait for A in a coffee shop, and it will not be that easy for A to locate B. Moreover, the search time will also be much greater compared to the earlier case. But here A has acted quite rationally in trying to minimise the search time and difficulty of finding B based on the information possessed.

This basically implies that rationality is not violated if something changes between their get-togethers, and the information regarding the change is not available to agents who are to take action. In this example, thus, we have considered a case of strategic interaction between person A and person B, where both their welfare levels (utility derived from meeting an old friend) are contingent on each other's actions, which therefore describes a game and illustrates how rationality is dependent on the level of information possessed by the individual agents involved in the game. We now more formally describe what exactly a game consists of.

Every game can be described in terms of five aspects:[6]

1 *The players:* Who are involved in playing the game?
2 *The action spaces:* What is the set of possible actions for a player?
3 *The rules:* Who moves when? What do they know when they move? What can they do?
4 *The outcomes:* For each possible set of actions by the players, what is the outcome of the game?
5 *The payoffs:* What are the players' preferences (i.e., utility functions) over the possible outcomes?

Games can be classified into different categories based broadly on two ways of categorisation: the number of times the players have to interact and the amount of information available to all players. Games that involve just once-and-for-all interaction among the players and are concluded after that are termed *static games* or *single-shot games*. The games that, on the other hand, involve multiple stages of interaction among the players are called *dynamic games*, *multiple-stage games*, *repeated games* or *sequential games*. The games where all the players have full information about one another and everyone knows this fact, where everyone knows that everyone knows this, and so on ad infinitum, which we formally call *common knowledge*, are known as *complete information games*. The name *game of incomplete information* itself suggests a lack of availability of information about some players. Now, both, the games of complete as well as incomplete information, can be static or dynamic.[7] For our purpose, we shall now concentrate on games of incomplete information.

In games of incomplete information, just like games of complete information, many agents interact with one another whose utilities are not just functions of their own actions but also depend on the actions chosen by all others. The only difference is that in the case of games of incomplete information, as opposed to games of complete information, the players do not know the types of the other players completely. This means that something about at least one player is exclusively known to that player alone and is not observable by others. Others will have some probabilistic notion about it. That is, whatever the factor about which a player possesses private information, others will only know what values this particular factor may have and with what probability each of these values will be acquired by the factor. Such probabilistic notion enables players to form expectations about others. The expectations are formed following the *Bayesian* rules of conditional probability. Thus, based on what a player observes about himself, the player calculates the expected values of factors not observable for the other players. This is why incomplete information games are also alternatively termed *Bayesian Games*. In Bayesian Games, as the players lack information about one another, they maximise expected utility rather than utility as is the case in complete information games. Thus the players choose strategies[8] based on the levels of information that they possess in order to maximise expected utilities.

Depending on the specifications of a game, the equilibrium strategies can always be worked out. For complete information games, the most effective equilibrium concept is that of *Nash equilibrium*. A Nash equilibrium strategy combination is the combination of strategies that, once reached, no player has any incentive to unilaterally deviate from. There may be more than one Nash equilibrium for certain games, and when a game actually has more than one Nash equilibrium, it cannot be predicted a priori which is more likely to prevail over the others. For static *Bayesian games*, the required equilibrium concept is that of *Bayesian Nash equilibrium*. This equilibrium involves not just the combination of strategies but also the beliefs of the players at equilibrium. This equilibrium is derived by maximising the expected utilities of all the players. Dynamic Bayesian games also involve a similar equilibrium concept known as the *Perfect Bayesian equilibrium*. This equilibrium concept shares some common features with the Bayesian Nash equilibrium in the sense that this also involves strategies and beliefs at equilibrium. This equilibrium is also derived by maximising the expected utilities of all the players. However, the Perfect Bayesian equilibrium also involves an additional feature, the idea of *sequential rationality*. This means that in games involving multiple stages, whenever it is time to choose an action, every player at each stage chooses the action that is considered optimum *given the level of information* that he possesses. Thus in the whole sequence of the game everywhere, all the players behave rationally. A *Perfect Bayesian equilibrium* is always characterised by sequential rationality. We also must note here that in dynamic Bayesian games, the beliefs of the players are updated at every stage, and the updating of beliefs plays a crucial role in ensuring sequential rationality.

Auctions as incomplete information games

With this background, we can now figure out how auctions can be formulated as incomplete information games. Just like any other incomplete information games, auctions involve players in the form of bidders and auctioneers who possess private information. Auctions are guided by rules, and, depending on the outcomes, the players derive payoffs. The bidders have the definite objective of maximising their respective expected utilities. This is true for procurement auctions also. These expected utilities may or may not be equal to the expected payoffs. Even when the expected utilities are not equal to expected payoffs, they will be monotonic functions of the expected payoffs. In auctions where the buyers are the bidders, the auctioneer may have various objectives like ensuring efficiency, maximising expected revenue or some combination of these two. In the case of procurement auctions, the auctioneer usually aims at obtaining either the best-quality product within a particular price range or obtaining the product of a fixed quality at the lowest possible price. In the case of scoring auctions, a combination of price and quality is considered in the form of a score following a predetermined formula, which was discussed in detail in Chapter 1.

To illustrate how auctions are formulated formally as incomplete information games, let us first consider an auction where the buyers are the bidders, there is a single seller who is also the auctioneer and a single object is up for sale. Let us suppose that there are N bidders. Every bidder has a privately known valuation for the object under consideration. For simplicity, we assume that the seller has zero valuation for the object.[9] The valuations of the bidders constitute their types, i.e., the maximum amount that a bidder is willing to bid defines the type of the bidder. If we consider the type of a bidder, only the concerned bidder knows her exact type (i.e., the maximum amount she is willing to bid); everyone else knows the probability distribution of her type, denoted by $F(\cdot)$, along with the interval over which the valuation is distributed. More specifically, this probability distribution function of valuation and this interval are common knowledge. How these types will be distributed depends on what assumption we make about the valuation framework. We now briefly discuss the basic notions of various valuation structures. Each of these cases can be found in reality, though not all the situations are equally prevalent. Some are more common while others, though rare, also exist in certain specific contexts. So, when we have to model auctions, it is helpful to have a notion about what the various valuation structures are and in what particular contexts they prevail.

Symmetric, independent, private valuations (SIPV)

First we consider a symmetric, independent, private valuation (SIPV) framework. Before proceeding into the analytical aspects of the model, let us explain what this nomenclature truly implies. In simplest terms, *independent values* means that no bidder's valuation for the object is impacted by any information about the other bidders' valuations.[10] *Independent, private valuation* indicates that the valuations of the bidders are independently distributed. Along with this, when the valuations of all the bidders are distributed following the same probability distribution function over the same interval, the corresponding framework becomes the SIPV framework. Here the bidders, though they differ in terms of their actual valuation for the object, are a priori symmetric. Hence we can select any bidder arbitrarily for the purpose of working out the equilibrium bid function, and since the bidders are symmetric a priori, the bid function at a symmetric equilibrium will be alike for all, though the actual bid values will be determined in terms of the valuations of individual bidders.[11] Most of the models studied in Auction Theory consider the SIPV framework since in many real-life cases, these assumptions seem logically plausible as well. Also, a very important contribution of the SIPV model is the famous *Revenue Equivalence Principle*. This principle states that under SIPV assumptions, when bidders are risk neutral, all the standard auction formats (i.e., the ones for which the highest-bidder-wins principle guides the selection of the winning bidder) are equivalent in terms of expected revenue. This means to say that in the ex ante sense, all the auction formats are likely to generate equal expected revenue, though ex post the actual revenue generated may very well vary across formats. The Revenue Equivalence Principle is discussed in detail in Chapter 4. However, revenue equivalence may not hold under certain circumstances. Some standard cases where the revenue equivalence may be violated are those of interdependent valuations in the presence of risk-averse or asymmetric bidders. The following sections illustrate these cases.

Allowing for interdependent values

There might be situations where the valuations of individual bidders are interdependent. This situation arises "when bidders have only partial information regarding the value, say in the form of a noisy signal".[12] In this case, other bidders may possess information that is likely to affect the valuation of an individual bidder for the object to be auctioned and hence the term *interdependent values*. Here, as mentioned earlier, the signals and the actual valuations differ from one another, though the valuation of an individual bidder is a function of the signal that the concerned bidder has. In technical terms, bidder i's signal is summarised as the random variable $X_i \in [0, \omega_i]$. The value that bidder i attaches to the object can be expressed as a function of all the bidders' signals as

$$V_i = v_i (X_1, X_2, ..., X_N)$$

The valuation of bidder i, i.e., v_i, is assumed to be strictly increasing in i's own signal X_i and non-decreasing in all the other variables X_j for $j = 1, 2, ..., N$ and $j \neq i$. For example, for higher bids from others, any bidder will always revise her valuation upwards or leave it at the current level. If values are expressed in this form, the underlying presumption is that there is no uncertainty and that value can be totally determined by the signals. However, more general forms can also be incorporated. Letting V_1, V_2, ... V_N denote the N values to bidders, which are unknown, $X_1, X_2, ..., X_N$; the N signals available to bidders and S a signal available to the seller, the expected value to bidder i, which is conditional on the information available to all the bidders, can be defined as

$$v_i\left(X_1, X_2, ..., X_N\right) \equiv E\left[V_i \mid X_1 = x_1, X_2 = x_2, ..., X_N = x_N\right]$$

Note that here the bidder i does not know his true valuation. All he knows is the signal (X_i) about his true valuation. This is true for all the bidders. Let bidder i get the signal x_i about his valuation. So, let $X_i = x_i$. This is again true for all the bidders. The preceding equation says that the expected value that bidder i attaches to the object under consideration (since he does not know the actual value) must be conditional on the signals that he and all the other bidders receive about their valuations. In other words, the expected valuation of bidder i is the expectation of the actual valuation of bidder i (which i does not know for sure), conditional on the signals that all the bidders receive, including bidder i. It is interesting to know that we have different models of interdependent valuations depending on the levels of information that bidder i possesses about the signals of all the other bidders. For example, in the case of common value, as discussed later in the chapter, it is known to all the bidders that all the bidders will get the same value ex post as a function of the signals they receive about the object. In a symmetric framework, these signals for individual bidders are distributed over the same interval following the same distribution function. In general it is presumed that

$$v_i\left(0, 0, ..., 0\right) = 0$$

and

$$E\left[V_i\right] < \infty$$

The first equation says that when all the bidders receive signals equal to 0, a bidder will believe that she has no value for the object. That is, if everybody else has no value for the object and she gets a signal that she also has no value for the object, then she believes that she must indeed have no value for the object.

The second condition says that valuations are finite. For example, one may think that the value of a person's life is infinite, i.e., one cannot judge the life of a person in terms of money. However, not everyone may feel this way. This can be best understood in the context of slave auctions. Evidences of slave auctions are historically documented. For example:

> *In early March 1859 an enormous slave auction took place at the Race Course three miles outside Savannah, Georgia. Four hundred thirty-six slaves were to be put on the auction block including men, women, children and infants. Word of the sale had spread through the South for weeks, drawing potential buyers from North and South Carolina, Virginia, Georgia, Alabama and Louisiana. All of Savannah's available hotel rooms and any other lodging spaces were quickly appropriated by the influx of visitors. In the days running up to the auction, daily excursions were made from the city to the Race Course to inspect, evaluate and determine an appropriate bid for the human merchandise on display.*[13]

This clearly suggests that human beings were treated just like any other inanimate merchandise items. Thus such cases provide support for the fact that whatever the object is that is up for sale, the valuations of the object for each of the bidders is finite, i.e., a bidder may have a sufficient amount of money to pay up to his valuation.

As long as the bidders are risk neutral, each bidder maximises the expected value of payoff $V_i - p_i$, where p_i is the price paid. When $v_i (X_1, X_2, \ldots X_N) = X_i$, we are back in the world of private values.

The signals, however, may or may not be distributed independently. Interdependence in valuations may occur in more than one ways. The two most common forms of interdependent values are common values and affiliation.

Common values are just the opposite extreme of private values. To define what common values are, let us consider a situation where the value of the object put up for auction will ex post be the same for all the bidders. But this value is not known to any of the bidders ex ante, i.e., when the bidders are bidding, they do not fully know exactly what value is going to materialise. This situation typically prevails in the case of bidding for the rights of exploration of some natural resource; for example, the value of oil available in a particular area for given international prices is fixed, but only after the successful bidder starts drilling is the value really known.[14] Prior to that, the bidders only have some expected estimates of this value, and they submit bids based on this expectation. In technical terms, if the signals to the bidders are expressed by the random variable $X_i \in [0,\omega]$, which are distributed independently following the same distribution function $F(\cdot)$ and a continuous density function $f(\cdot)$ (in a symmetric framework). For the case of *pure common values*, the value of the object to bidder i, V_i, can be expressed as a function of all bidders' signals as

$$V = v\left(X_1, X_2, ..., X_N\right)$$

Since the only information available to any individual bidder is her own signal, despite the ex post value being the same for all, for analytical purposes as well as practical interests, first a distribution of the common value V is specified, and it is assumed that bidders' signals X_i are independently distributed conditional on the event $V = v$. More specifically every individual signal X_i is assumed to be an unbiased estimator of V, which means that $E[X_i \mid V = v] = v$.

In the context of common values, the issue of the *winner's curse* is worth mentioning.[15] Since preceding an auction, an individual bidder i only observes his own signal $X_i = x$, therefore the estimated value based solely on this information is $E[V \mid X_i = x]$. If in this framework when bidders are symmetric, a first price sealed bid auction is conducted, and the bids are announced post auction, the winning bidder i realises that the signals received by all the remaining bidders are less than x. Hence, this announcement suggests that bidder i had initially overestimated the value. Therefore, despite winning the auction, the inability to rightly estimate the value while formulating the bidding strategy effectively implies that the winner ends up paying more than the worth of the object. This phenomenon is known as the *winner's curse*, so named since in such situations, winning itself brings in the feeling of being cursed. However, it needs to be noted here that *winner's curse* is a disequilibrium situation, and thus it does not prevail at equilibrium.

So far we have assumed the bidders' signals to be independently distributed. However, the bidders' signals may very well be correlated. When the correlation is positive and the degree of correlation is very high such that some X_i values being very high implies that the other remaining X_i values are also high, it is said that the signals X_1, X_2, ..., X_N are affiliated. In the case of *affiliation*, the joint density of the signals X_1, X_2, ..., X_N expressed by $f(X_1, X_2, ..., X_N)$ is no longer the product of the individual densities as was the case for independently distributed signals.

Allowing for risk-averse bidding behaviour

When bidders are risk neutral, maximisation of the expected utility of payoff and the maximisation of the expected payoff are one and the same. However, in reality many bidders may be risk averse. Suppose, in a single object auction, the buyer whose valuation is v wins and pays p to the seller. Then the payoff of the buyer is $(v - p)$. However, the concerned bidder's utility is $u(v - p)$, where $u(\cdot)$ is a non-decreasing function. The objective of each of the bidders is to maximise her own expected utility. If the bidder is risk neutral, then the expected utility maximisation can be replaced with the expected profit maximisation. The risk behaviour of the bidders affects the bidding strategies in many significant ways. For example, although the Revenue Equivalence Principle holds for risk-neutral bidders, it does not hold for risk-averse bidders. In particular, we have the following result:

> **Result:** *Suppose that bidders are risk-averse with the same utility function. With symmetric, independent private values, the expected revenue in a first-price auction is greater than that in a second-price auction.*

Allowing for asymmetries among bidders

So far, whatever deviations from the standard SIPV framework have been considered, one aspect has been common for all, which is the assumption that bidders are a priori symmetric. However, even this may not always be the case. The bidders may be asymmetric ex ante. This happens when different bidders' values are drawn from different probability distributions over the same interval or same probability distribution over different intervals or different probability distributions over different intervals. In the most general form, this can be stated as bidder i's valuation X_i being distributed over $[0,\omega_i]$, following distribution function F_i with density f_i. This means that bidder 1's valuation X_1 is distributed over $[0,\omega_1]$, following distribution function F_1 with density f_1; bidder 2's valuation X_1 is distributed over $[0,\omega_2]$ following distribution function F_2 with density f_2, and so on. Thus bidder N's valuation X_N is distributed over $[0,\omega_N]$ following distribution function F_N with density f_N. The bidders may be risk neutral or risk averse. If they are risk neutral, then they will maximise the expected payoff, whereas if they are risk averse, they will maximise the expected utility of payoff. But when bidders are ex ante asymmetric, the objective functions will no longer be alike, and hence *we cannot select any representative bidder* to calculate the general bid function. Instead, we have to calculate specific bid functions for the specific bidders.

Modelling multiple object auctions

Modelling of multiple object auctions is mostly analogous to their single object counterparts. However, here, instead of a single valuation for any individual bidder, we have a valuation vector for the concerned bidder.

There are many examples of multiple object auctions. Treasury bills, shares of a company, radio spectrums etc. are all examples of multiple object auctions. Treasury bills are sold through public auctions in countries like the United States and India to finance public debt. Auctioning shares, which takes place at Bombay Stock Exchange (BSE) and National Stock Exchange (NSE), is quite common in India. The auction of the radio spectrum is quite well known worldwise since many countries are using auctions for allocating licenses to use the radio spectrum, and day by day more countries are joining this club.[16] At times in auction houses in privately conducted auctions, certain items are offered for sale together, especially when they are substitutes or complements. Examples include pieces of furniture or utensils. Some wooden antique chairs manufactured in the same batch may be put up for sale together, perhaps complemented by a wooden table also manufactured at the same time as the chairs. Tea sets consisting of tea pots and cups may be offered for sale together. There may also be cases where a series of paintings by an eminent artist, which follow a definite sequence (rooted in mythology or some historical incident), are put up for auction together. These items may be offered as stand-alone objects or may be clubbed together as packages. The bidding behaviour of bidders and thus the revenue prospects may vary depending on how the objects are related to one another and whether they are offered for sale separately or in packages.

Multiple object auctions can be represented theoretically as follows: if there are K objects (where $K \geq 2$), for an individual bidder i, the valuation vector will be denoted by $V^i = \left(V_1^i, V_2^i, ..., V_K^i\right)$. Now, if there are N bidders, we will have a total of $N \times K$ values. Accordingly, we will have a total of $N \times K$ bids, where the bid vector for the individual bidder i will be $\beta^i = \left(\beta_1^i, \beta_2^i, ..., \beta_K^i\right)$. If we are in a symmetric framework, the bid functions for all the bidders will be identical, though bid values will be different depending on the individual valuations for the objects. The calculation of bid functions, however, is generally much more complex when multiple objects are involved. The calculations of bid functions under various contexts are dealt with in detail in Chapter 4.

Notes

1 Here *auctioneers* refers to the agents who on behalf of the sellers design and conduct the auction, while sellers are just the suppliers of the objects, who earn revenues by offering their possessions for sale. The sellers may pay the auctioneers some pre-agreed amount as remuneration for their service. When the sellers design and conduct the auctions themselves, then the sellers and auctioneers are one and the same. There is no hard and fast rule regarding this distinction between sellers and auctioneers. In fact, in an alternative opinion, sellers are

always to be regarded as auctioneers, and the agents they recruit for designing and/or conducting the auctions on their behalf are to be perceived as intermediaries facilitating the process of auction.

2 This distinction has been also mentioned in Chapter 1 of this book.

3 These classifications were discussed in detail in Chapter 1.

4 Double auctions are very complicated games for which the determination of bid functions is not as simple as in the case of auctions with one-sided private information. Detailed discussion on double auctions is not provided here. Interested readers may look up Chatterjee and Samuelson (1983) for a theoretical discussion on double auction.

5 Mas-Colell, Whinston and Green (2006).

6 These aspects are described fully following Mas-Colell, Whinston and Green (2006).

7 The games of complete information can be further classified into two categories: games of perfect information and games of imperfect information. When all the players can observe the full history of the game at every stage, i.e., what actions have been chosen by the players at every stage, then the game is one of perfect information. However, even if just one player is unable to observe even one part of the history, the game becomes one of imperfect information. Harsanyi (1967) established a theoretical equivalence between games of imperfect information and games of incomplete information.

8 A strategy in *Game Theory* is defined to be a complete, contingent plan of action (Mas-Colell, Whinston and Green, 2006). This means that a player, while choosing an action, considers all the possibilities or contingencies that may arise and, depending on these possibilities, decides which action is to be optimally chosen under what contingency. Thus the choice of a strategy is contingent on the different situations that may possibly arise, and each player considers all the possibilities she can foresee.

9 This assumption is a simplifying assumption when the seller has a fixed valuation for the object that is common knowledge and thus does not make any significant difference to the results derived. However, this same assumption differentiates the simple auction from the double auction. If the seller also has a privately known valuation for the object, then the nature of the analysis changes substantially.

10 Though the exact valuations of other bidders are not observable beforehand, the information about probability distribution of other bidders is always common knowledge.

11 The equilibrium bid functions are calculated assuming that all the bidders bid truthfully; i.e., they submit bids as functions of their true valuations, and thus it can be proved following the usual procedure that any individual bidder will also bid on the basis of his true valuation at a symmetric equilibrium and that no bidder has any incentive to deviate unilaterally from this bidding behaviour.

12 Krishna (2010).

13 www.eyewitnesstohistory.com/slaveauction.htm

14 Menezes and Monteiro (2008).

15 The historical background for such a nomenclature has been elaborated in Chapter 1.

16 Radio or telecom spectrum auctions are discussed in detail in Chapters 5 and 6.

4 Some standard results in Auction Theory

Modelling auctions as incomplete information games have led to the birth of some results that bear direct relevance to real-life policymaking. Some such important results (one of them being the famous Revenue Equivalence Theorem) are described here, along with elaborations on their applications to real-life policy choices.

Some common auction types

Auction formats can be broadly categorised into two types, open auctions and sealed bid auctions. In *open auctions*, bidders bid openly so that every bidder gets to see how much others bid. In this case, after each round of bidding, the remaining bidders revise their strategy for bidding, i.e., whether to continue bidding or to drop out. Open auctions usually have multiple rounds of bidding. Only when the auction is concluded do we have the equilibrium bid or bids depending on whether we are having a single unit or a multiple unit auction. All other interim bids are disequilibrium bids. Sealed bid auctions are usually single stage auctions. In sealed bid auctions, each bidder submits a bid in a sealed envelope, and no bidder can observe what everybody else is bidding. In both, open as well as sealed bid auctions, an individual bidder's equilibrium bid depends on some private information that the concerned bidder possesses, i.e., the information that the bidder possesses exclusively. Usually this would be the valuation that each bidder attaches to the object. When an individual bidder's bid is solely dependent on the concerned bidder's valuation irrespective of what the concerned bidder observes about her contenders, we are in the world of independent valuation. On the other hand, when a bidder's valuation depends on whatever information she possesses about the other bidders' valuations, the framework is that of interdependent valuation.[1] In the case of open auctions, the scope for revising valuations about objects is larger compared to sealed bid formats since in the former, the bidders are able to fully observe their contenders' bidding behaviour.

In this chapter, we discuss in detail some major open and sealed bid auction formats for both single unit as well as multiple unit auctions. In the category of single unit auctions, we look at four major auction formats, viz., English Auction, Dutch Auction, first price sealed bid auction and second price sealed bid auction. Among these, English and Dutch Auctions are open auctions while first and second price sealed bid auctions are sealed bid auctions, as the names suggest. In the case of multiple unit auctions, the most standard sealed bid auctions are discriminatory or pay-your-bid auction and the Uniform Price Auction. English and Dutch Auctions are the open auction formats used in the case of multiple unit auctions as well.

English Auction is the most commonly known auction format. The sale of antique items, paintings, art objects etc. at Sotheby's or Christie's is done through English Auctions. This is an ascending price open auction. In an English Auction for a single object, typically, an auctioneer (who may be the seller) announces a price low enough such that more than one buyer shows interest in buying the object at that price. Then the auctioneer raises the price, to see how many buyers are still interested in buying the object at the new price. This process continues until at a particular price only one buyer remains who is willing to buy the object at that price. This is the price where the second-to-last bidder drops out. If it so happens that more than one, suppose two, bidders remain interested in the object and they drop out together at the same price, then there has to be a suitable tie-breaking rule, which needs to be announced beforehand. Intuitively it is clear that since no buyer will be interested in buying the object by paying an amount of money more than his own valuation, the price at which the object is finally sold is the valuation of the buyer with the second highest valuation.

The Dutch Auction is an open descending price auction. It has its roots in the seventeenth-century Dutch flower markets.[2] It continues to be in use for the auction of flowers. The flower auction at Aalsmeer, Netherlands, is the largest flower auction in the world, where 20 million flowers, originating in different countries like Ecuador, Colombia, Ethiopia, Kenya and also several parts of Europe, are sold every day.[3] It is different from English Auction in the sense that here the prices are revised downwards as opposed to upwards as in the case of English Auctions. Here again there is an auctioneer, who starts by declaring a very high price for the object. If no bidder displays willingness to buy the object at that price, the auctioneer reduces the price to see whether anybody shows interest in buying the object at that revised price. This downward revision of prices continues until at least one bidder shows interest. The auction ends at the price where only one bidder shows interest in buying the object. In this case also, there needs to be a suitable pre-announced tie-breaking rule in the case more than one bidders are interested in buying the object at a particular price. However, this auction is not so commonly used in practice for selling a single unit, but it is quite useful for multiple object auctions.[4] The Treasury bill auction in the United States, conducted by the United States Department of the Treasury through the Federal Reserve Bank of New York, is done through Dutch Auction. The Initial Public Offering (IPO) of companies (the first sale of stocks issued by a company to the public[5]) is quite often conducted through Dutch Auctions. Company shares are also sold through Dutch Auctions.

In a sealed bid auction, as the name suggests, the bidders must submit bids in sealed envelopes, such that no other bidder knows the bid of a particular bidder. In the case of first price sealed bid auction, the bidder whose bid is the highest wins the auction and pays his own bid. In a sealed bid second price auction, again the highest bidder wins the auction but pays the highest losing bid, i.e., the winner pays the second highest bid.

Now under certain assumptions, some equivalences may be observed between open and sealed bid auctions. More specifically, under the usual assumptions of symmetric independent private valuations, the first price sealed bid auction and the Dutch Auction are equivalent, while the second price sealed bid auction is equivalent to English Auction. This is important because a seller will then be indifferent between choosing an open or a sealed bid auction. For example, because of these equivalences, the expected revenue to the seller by choosing first price sealed bid auction is equal to the Dutch open auction. Another important factor here is that since open auctions are dynamic auctions where only the final bids are the equilibrium bids while all the interim bids are disequilibrium bids, due to the equivalence between open and sealed bid auctions, we can calculate the equilibrium bidding strategies for open auctions from the calculations for sealed bid auctions without much difficulty. The following section elaborates on these equivalence relations between open and sealed bid auction formats.

Equivalence between different auction formats

In this section, we discuss the strategic equivalence between certain auction formats. Two auction formats are strategically equivalent when, given all other things to be constant, each outcome of one auction can be replicated by another auction with a suitably chosen strategy. That is, for each outcome in one auction, there exists a strategy in the other auction that results in the same outcome.

We first show that Dutch Auction and the first price sealed bid auction are strategically equivalent. Though it may sound a bit surprising to start with, a close look at the dynamics of bidding in the Dutch Auction helps in clarifying this. The auctioneer keeps quoting prices and asks bidders whether they are willing to pay the quoted price to get the object and keeps revising it downward until at least one bidder shows interest. The downward revision of prices can be done in a continuum using some price clock. When a bidder actually responds positively, it means that the quoted price is matching the concerned bidder's maximum willingness to pay for the object under consideration. This price is therefore nothing but the highest bid that the bidder will be quoting given an option to bid. Now, in a first price sealed bid auction, a buyer bids only using her own private information. Although the Dutch Auction is open, the openness does not provide any extra information to any buyers as long we are in the independent valuation framework. All that the buyers can observe is that at some particular quoted price, only one buyer agrees to buy the object. But the auction ends immediately, so this information is useless to the rest of the buyers. Thus, in Dutch Auctions, the buyers must bid depending on their own private information only. So suppose a buyer bids b in the first price auction, then in the Dutch Auction, that buyer will agree to buy the object if the price is b or less. Therefore, strategically the equilibrium bid in a Dutch Auction is effectively the highest bid in a first price sealed bid auction.

In the case of the private value model, the English Auction and the second price sealed bid auction are also strategically equivalent. In English Auctions, bidders get eliminated as the price quoted by the auctioneer keeps being revised upwards. The upward revision of prices can also be done in a continuum using a price clock. Thus when only one bidder remains, the last one to drop out is basically the bidder whose valuation for the object is exactly matched by the price quoted by the auctioneer. Since the auction is concluded at this point, the price that the winning bidder has to pay is nothing but the second highest valuation. In a second price sealed bid auction, the winning bidder must pay the second highest bid. Although one may think that knowing at what prices the buyers are dropping out adds some extra information to the existing buyers, since the valuation is private, this provides no extra useful information to a participating buyer. Thus the equilibrium bid in the English Auction is also the bid in the second price sealed bid auction, and these two formats are strategically equivalent. However, this equivalence depends crucially on the assumption of the private valuation. If the valuation is not private, this equivalence between second price sealed bid auction and English Auction does not hold. This aspect is discussed subsequently in this chapter.

In the next section, we discuss the single object auctions in detail, considering the various contingencies regarding the valuations of bidders.[6]

Single object auctions

The symmetric model

The principal features of the symmetric independent private valuation model have been discussed in detail in Chapter 3. Now we proceed to analyse the equilibrium bidding behaviour for first and second price sealed bid auctions in the SIPV framework. We consider the case where only one seller is selling a single object through auction. There are $N > 1$ potential buyers, bidding for the object. Buyer i's valuation (the maximum amount of money that the buyer is willing to pay) for the object is V_i. Each valuation is independently and identically distributed on some interval $[0, \omega]$ according to an increasing and continuous distribution function $F(\cdot)$. The corresponding density function is $f(\cdot)$ We assume that $E(V) < \infty$.[7]

Now V_i is a random variable. Only buyer i knows the realised value v_i of V_i and that the valuations of other buyers are independently distributed according to $F(\cdot)$. All the buyers are risk neutral. This means that their objective is to maximise their own expected profits.[8] All components of the model other than the realised values are assumed to be commonly known to all the bidders. No bidder faces any budget constraint. This means that every bidder can afford to pay whatever bid she quotes. We first analyse the second price sealed bid auction and then proceed to discuss the first price sealed bid auction.

Second price sealed bid auction

In a second price sealed bid auction, each buyer submits a bid (b_i for buyer i) for the object. The highest bidder wins the auction. In exchange for the object, the winner must pay the second highest bid as per rules of the auction. The losing bidders pay nothing.

Thus the payoff of the buyer i can be expressed as

$$
\Pi_i = \begin{cases} v_i - \max_{i \neq j} b_j & \text{if } b_i > \max_{j \neq i} b_j \\ 0 & \text{if } b_i < \max_{j \neq i} b_j \end{cases}
$$

Note that b_j is the bid of the jth bidder, so $\max_{j \neq i} b_j$ is the highest bid excluding the bid of bidder i. If $b_i < \max_{j \neq i} b_j$ holds, then at least one other bidder bids more than does bidder i, so bidder i will not win the auction, and therefore her profit will be zero. However, if $b_i > \max_{j \neq i} b_j$ holds, then bidder i is the highest bidder, so she wins the auction and pays the second highest bid (which is nothing but $\max_{j \neq i} b_j$). So her profit is her valuation net of her payment (i.e., $v_i - \max_{j \neq i} b_j$).

Finally, we assume that if there is a tie, then the object goes to each winning bidder with equal probability.

The following Result 1 gives us the equilibrium bidding behaviour of the bidders.

Result 1: *In a symmetric increasing equilibrium, every buyer will bid his own true valuation in a second price sealed bid auction.*

This result is quite intuitive and can be proved very simply without difficulty. We proceed by supposing that buyer i bids p_1, which is higher than v_i. Let us denote the second highest bid by p_2. Suppose the bidder wins the auction. Now if $p_2 > v_i$ holds, then the bidder will incur loss. However if the bidder bids his own valuation, then he loses the auction and will incur no loss since no payment accrues to the losing bidders. If on the other hand $v_i > p_2$, then bidding b_1 or v_i will yield the profit equal to $v_i - p_2$. So the bidder is indifferent between bidding b_1 or v_i. Thus overbidding involves no possibility of gain; rather, in one particular case, it involves a possibility of loss. So the buyer will never overbid in a second price sealed bid auction.

Now suppose the bidder bids less than his true value, that is, $b_1 < v_i$. If $b_1 > p_2$; then the bidder will win irrespective of whether he bids b_1 or v_i. So here the bidder is indifferent between bidding b_1 and v_i. However, if the bidder loses and $b_1 < p_2 < v_i$ holds, then the bidder faces a payoff equal to zero. However, bidding his own valuation results in a payoff equal to $v_i - p_2 > 0$. So also in the case of underbidding, there is no possibility of gain, and in one particular case there is a possibility of loss. So the bidder will never underbid in a second price sealed bid auction.

Combining the above two cases, we can easily figure out that in the case of second price sealed bid auction, a bidder will always bid her true valuation. If an auction allocates the object to a bidder who values the object most, we say the auction is *efficient*. Note that the seller or auctioneer does not know which bidder has the highest valuation beforehand. But still the seller or auctioneer can design an auction (for example, we see the second price sealed bid auction is efficient) that can allocate the object to the bidder who has the highest valuation for the object and thus ensure ex-post efficiency. Efficiency is a major concern for the government, particularly for the allocation of scare natural resources (for example, spectrum, coal mines, oil fields etc.) to private parties.

Thus the expected payment by a bidder whose valuation is v in a second price sealed bid auction is given by

$$m^{II}(v) = Prob(Win) \times E(2\text{nd highest bid right} \mid v \text{ is the highest bid})$$

$$= G(v) \times E(Y_1 \mid Y_1 < v)$$

Here Y_1 denotes the highest valuation among the rest of the bidders, and $G(y) = F^{N-1}(y)$ is the distribution function of Y_1. In words, the expected payment by a bidder whose valuation is v is the expected second highest valuation, given v is the highest valuation, multiplied by the probability that v is indeed the highest valuation.

First price sealed bid auction

In first price sealed bid auction, each bidder submits a bid (b_i for bidder i) for the object. The highest bidder wins the auction. In exchange for the object, the winner must pay her own bid. Here also the losing bidders pay nothing.

The payoff of the bidder i is given by

$$\Pi_i = \begin{cases} v_i - b_i & \text{if } b_i > \max\limits_{j \neq i} b_j \\ 0 & \text{if } b_i < \max\limits_{j \neq i} b_j \end{cases}$$

Finally, we assume that in the case of a tie, the object goes to each winning bidder with equal probability.

The equilibrium bidding strategy in a first price sealed bid auction is more complicated compared to that in a second price sealed bid auction. First note that no bidder will bid more than or equal to her own valuation, since in the case of winning, the bidder must pay her bid, which then is greater than or equal to her valuation for the object. In this case, the bidder either incurs a loss or at best obtains a zero payoff.

However, the higher the bid, the higher the probability is of winning, but at the same time the less the payoff is. On the other hand, the less the bid amount, the less the probability is of winning and the greater the payoff is. The bidder, being risk neutral, is maximising her own expected payoff, which is nothing but the payoff multiplied by the probability of winning. The symmetric equilibrium bid function is obtained by maximising this expected payoff, and its explicit form is stated in the following Result 2.

Result 2: *Symmetric equilibrium bidding strategy in a first price sealed bid auction is given by*

$$b(v) = E\left(Y_1 \mid Y_1 < v\right)$$

In other words, a bidder whose valuation is v will bid the amount that is the expected valuation of the second highest bidder given that her valuation is the highest valuation.

Suppose the valuations are distributed uniformly over the interval [0,1]. Here $F(y) = y$ and $G(y) = y^{N-1}$. So we have $b(v) = \dfrac{N-1}{N}v$. The amount of bid shading is $\dfrac{v}{N}$. Note that in the case of a second price sealed bid auction, there is no bid shading.

The expected payment by a bidder whose valuation is v, is given by

$$m^I(v) = G(v) \times E\left(Y_1 \mid Y_1 < v\right)$$

Note that this is exactly equal to that for the second price sealed bid auction. So let $m(v) = m^I(v) = m^{II}(v)$ Also, the expected revenue to the seller in both auctions is

$$E(R) = N\int_0^{\omega} m(v)\,dv$$

This is a very useful result, which is also relevant for real-life policymaking regarding choice of auction formats. In fact, this is a famous result that establishes the fact that under the SIPV assumption, first and second price sealed bid auctions yield the same expected revenue to the seller.[9] The following Result 3 states it formally.

> **Result 3:** *For symmetric bidders, with independently and identically distributed private values, the expected revenue in a first price sealed bid auction is the same as the expected revenue in a second price sealed bid auction.*

This theorem is a restricted version of a more general theorem, called the *revenue equivalence theorem*. This theorem is robust in the sense that even if we introduce reserve prices, the two auction formats yield exactly equal amounts of expected revenue to the seller.

Note that the effect of reserve price and entry fee is the same for these two auction formats. That is, the revenue a seller secures by introducing a reserve price can also be generated by suitably choosing an entry fee. More precisely, suppose $r > 0$ is the amount of reserve price. The equilibrium bidding will not change if, instead of reserve price, we introduce $e > 0$ amount of entry fee, where $e = G(r) \times r$. Note that since $0 < G(r) < 1$, we have $e > r$.

However, there is an efficiency–revenue tradeoff when a seller introduces reserve price (or entry fee). That is, by introducing reserve price, the seller may lose efficiency. For example, suppose the valuation of the seller is 0 for simplicity. Without a reserve price (or entry fee), the bidder who has the highest valuation wins the auction. Now that bidder clearly values the object more than the seller does. However, suppose now there is a reserve price of amount r. Clearly, those bidders whose valuations are greater than zero but less than r will not participate in the auction. If all the bidders' valuations lie in this interval, then the object will remain unsold even if there are bidders whose valuations are more than the seller's valuation. Clearly this is inefficient because the object does not reach the buyer who values it the most. As noted earlier, governments are mostly concerned about efficiency in allocation, whereas private players are mostly concerned about the amount of revenue generation. But even governments may consider revenue generation as the second important objective after efficiency. In such cases, governments may choose from efficient auction formats and select the one that generates the highest expected revenue. However, due to Theorem 3, we can infer that given an option to choose, the government will be indifferent between first and second price sealed bid auctions when efficiency and revenue are the prime considerations.[10]

Revenue equivalence theorem

In the preceding section, we saw that the expected revenues generated to the seller by a first price sealed bid auction and a second price sealed bid auction are exactly equal. In this section, we will see that this revenue equivalence holds for a large class of auctions, known as *standard auctions*. A standard auction is basically the auction where the highest bidder is the winning bidder. We formally state the Revenue Equivalence Principle in the following Result 4.

> **Result 4:** *Suppose that values are symmetrically, independently and identically distributed and that all bidders are risk neutral. Then any symmetric and increasing equilibrium of any standard auction, such that the expected payment of a bidder with value zero is zero, yields the same expected revenue to the seller.*

This theorem says that the expected revenue generated will always be equal to

$$E(R) = N \int_0^\omega m(v) \, dv$$

where $m(v) = \times E(Y_1 | Y_1 < v)$.

Let us consider a specific example where valuations are distributed uniformly over the interval $[0,1]$. Then the expected revenue is

$$E(R) = \frac{N-1}{N+1}$$

Note that, first, in the case of uniform distribution of valuations over the interval [0,1], the expected revenue to seller depends only on the number of buyers and nothing else. Second, as the number of buyers rises, the expected revenue will also rise. This is the usual effect of competition. As more buyers compete for a single object, their bid shading is less.

Revenue equivalence theorem can be used to find out the bidding strategies of many uncommon auctions. One such example is the *all pay auction*. In an all pay auction, every bidder must pay his bid irrespective of winning. The equilibrium bidding strategy for an all pay auction is given by

$$b(v) = \int_0^v y dG(y) = G(v) \times E\left(Y_1 \mid Y_1 < v\right)$$

Clearly, the expected revenue to the seller is N times the bid.

Interestingly, there are auctions where a bidder may bid *more* than his own valuation. One such example is third price sealed bid auction. Here, as usual, the highest bidder wins but pays the third highest bid. The equilibrium bidding strategy is given by

$$b(v) = v + \frac{F(v)}{(N-2)f(v)}$$

Note that $(N-2)$ is positive because, as there is the third highest bid, the number of bidders must be greater than or equal to three. Here, as one can see, $\frac{F(v)}{(N-2)f(v)} > 0$, which means $b(v) > v$.

Extensions of the SIPV model

The SIPV model assumes many restrictions on bidders; for example, bidders are risk neutral, they have no budget constraints and their valuations are independently distributed according to the same distribution function. In this section, we will relax those assumptions one at a time and see how bidding behaviour changes and whether revenue equivalence theorem still holds.

Risk-averse buyers

Suppose we relax the risk neutrality assumption and assume that the bidders are risk averse.[11] This is commonly observed for auctions of perishable goods of a heterogeneous nature. One ready example is that of fish auctions. Here the buyers are typically risk averse[12] for more than one reason: first, they are not sure of the exact combination of the different types of fishes in a lot when the fishes are clubbed together; second, if for some reason the resale of the fish in the markets does not go well, the preservation of the fish will prove costly; third, due to unexpected shocks, the demands for different types of fishes may differ quite substantially from expected levels; fourth, the fish sellers in the markets are usually not very rich and possess limited resources, so they are a little extra careful about the risk involved in the resale process of fish compared to rich traders. However, despite allowing for risk-averse bidders, we retain all the other assumptions of the previous setup. What this implies is that the von Neumann–Morgenstern utility function of a buyer $u(\cdot)$ is strictly increasing and strictly convex.

Result 5 shows that unfortunately the revenue equivalence theorem does not hold when buyers are risk averse.

Result 5: *Suppose that bidders are risk averse with the same utility function. With symmetric, independent private values, the expected revenue in a first price sealed bid auction is greater than that in a second price sealed bid auction.*

Note that in the case of the second price sealed bid auction, for a buyer, it is still the equilibrium strategy to report her valuation truthfully as a bid because the intuition we have given does not depend on whether the buyer is risk neutral or risk averse. However, the equilibrium bidding strategy for first price sealed bid auction changes due to the change in the risk behaviour. In particular, bidders will bid more aggressively in first price sealed bid auction.

The reason is the following: consider a risk-averse bidder who bids b in a first price sealed bid auction. Now if the same bidder bids slightly less than b and wins the auction, then the concerned bidder will pay slightly less and therefore her utility will rise slightly. However, due to low bidding, her probability of winning is also less. A risk-averse bidder will lay more emphasis on the probability of winning as opposed to slightly higher utility. So the bidder will bid more to ensure a higher probability of winning. This means that a risk-averse bidder will bid more aggressively than a risk-neutral bidder in a first price sealed bid auction, thus resulting in higher expected revenue.

Budget constraint

Here we assume buyers have a fixed amount of money to spend rather than an unlimited amount of money as assumed in earlier sections. This is also quite realistic since other than a few millionaires, usually bidders possess limited resources, and this phenomenon bears definite impact on the bidding behaviour. We assume each buyer's valuation and wealth pair (V_i, W_i) is distributed independently and identically on $[0,1] \times [0,1]$ according to the distribution function $F(\cdot)$, which has the density function $f(\cdot)$. Only bidder i knows the realised valuation and wealth i.e., (v_i, w_i). We again assume that bidders are risk neutral. It is important to note that in all earlier situations, it was always the case that a bidder has one-dimensional private information only. However, in this case, every bidder has two-dimensional private information, viz., her valuation and amount of wealth she has.

This is probably the only instance where the bidding strategy of the second price sealed bid auction differs from its usual form of bidding true valuation. This is formally stated in Result 6.

Result 6: *In a second price sealed bid auction, it is an equilibrium strategy to bid according to $b(v, w) = min\{v, w\}$.*

Note that when $w \geq v$, the equilibrium bidding strategy is $b(v,w) = v$, which is also the equilibrium bidding strategy of the usual SIPV model. The equilibrium bidding strategy changes only when $w < v$. Here a buyer is unable to pay up to her own valuation, so the best she can do is to bid w, which is the maximum amount she can afford to pay and is closest to her valuation.

We assume that in the case of first price sealed bid auction, a symmetric equilibrium of the form $b(v,w) = min\{\beta(v), w\}$ exists, where $\beta(\cdot)$ is an increasing function. Then the next result claims that, when bidders face budget constraints, the Revenue Equivalence Principle may not work.

Result 7: *Suppose that bidders are subject to financial constraints. If the first price sealed bid auction has a symmetric equilibrium of the form $b(v, w) = min\{\beta(v), w\}$, then the expected revenue in a first price sealed bid auction is greater than the expected revenue in a second price sealed bid auction.*

Asymmetric bidders

Finally, assume that the bidders are asymmetric in the sense that the valuations of the bidders are distributed according to different distribution functions.[13] So the valuations are not identically distributed. The rest of the assumptions are identical to the symmetry model.

Several observations can be made. First, it is still optimal for a bidder to bid his own valuation in the second price sealed bid auction. The reason is rooted in the way we derive the equilibrium bidding strategy in a second price sealed bid auction – we do not assume anything about the distribution function of valuations of the bidders. Second, in the case of the first price sealed bid auction, although it can be shown that an equilibrium bidding strategy exists, there is no closed form solution for it. Therefore, we know only that an equilibrium bidding strategy exists, but we do not know exactly what it is. Finally, the second price sealed bid auction is still efficient here, though first price sealed bid auction is no longer efficient. So here also the revenue equivalence theorem does not hold. However, an interesting result is famously quoted in the literature: "weakness leads to aggression", as is now illustrated.

Suppose there are only two bidders 1 and 2. X_1 is distributed according to the distribution function F_1 in the interval $[0,\omega_1]$. And X_2 is distributed according to the distribution function F_2 in the interval $[0,\omega_2]$. We assume $\omega_1 > \omega_2$. We say bidder 2 is weak if F_1 stochastically dominates F_2 in terms of reverse hazard rate. That is, for all $v \in (0,\omega_2)$, we have

$$\frac{f_1(v)}{F_1(v)} > \frac{f_2(v)}{F_2(v)}$$

Result 8 establishes the fact that the bidder whose value is dominated in terms of the reverse hazard rate will bid more aggressively.

Result 8: *Suppose that the value distribution of bidder 1 dominates that of bidder 2 in terms of the reverse hazard rate. Then in a first price auction, the "weak" bidder 2 bids more aggressively than the "strong" bidder 1; that is, for all $v \in (0, \omega_2)$, we have $b_1(v) < b_2(v)$, where $b_1(v)$ is the equilibrium bidding strategy for buyer 1, and $b_2(v)$ is that of for buyer 2.*

Finally in the case of revenue comparison, as stated earlier, the revenue equivalence theorem does not hold. Worse still is that no general ranking is possible between the revenue of the first price sealed bid auction and the second price sealed bid auction. Sometimes the first price sealed bid auction generates higher expected revenue than the second price sealed bid auction. And other times the opposite occurs.

Auctions with interdependent valuations

We first drop the independent value assumption. In previous section, we assumed that the valuation of one buyer does not depend on what other buyers think about the object. That is, the valuation of one buyer does not depend on the signals that the other buyers have. So here the valuation of one bidder depends on the signals of all the other bidders regarding the object up for sell. Thus one does not know her valuation fully. So the valuations are no longer private, but a part of the valuation is private and the rest is simply unknown. This scenario is quite common for auctions of antique items. The aspiring buyers may be uncertain whether a painting by Michelangelo or van Gogh is genuine, or whatever stories are told about why a particular item is rare may be fabricated, and the potential buyers may not possess enough information individually to verify the extent of truth in it. In such cases, every bidder observes how other bidders behave or what they say and continuously revises her valuation of the concerned object. The scope for doing so is, of course, higher for open auctions.

In the case of interdependent valuations, each buyer receives some private signals regarding the object. Let that private information of buyer i be the realisation of the random variable $X_i \in [0,\omega_i]$. So the valuation of buyer i is $v_i = V_i(X_1,...,X_N)$. The function V_i is non-decreasing in all its variables and at least twice continuously differentiable. Finally V_i is strictly increasing in X_i.

Note that, first, our earlier private valuation model is a special case of this interdependent valuation model. In that case, the buyers have private valuation, and we write $v_i = V_i(X_i)$. Second, suppose all the buyers place the same value on the object but do not know that exact value (consider an auction of an oil deposit; each buyer will get the same amount of oil subject to winning the auction yet does not know how much oil there is in the deposit). That is, the final value is the same irrespective of who wins, but it is unknown to all the buyers. This type of model is known as the *common value* model. This is another extreme case of the interdependent value model.

English Auction vs. second price sealed bid auction

We have already stated that under the assumption of symmetry, English Auction and second price sealed bid auction are equivalent. However, under interdependent valuations, they are not. The reason is simple. In the case of the second price sealed bid auction, a buyer gets no information about the private information of all the other bidders in the bidding process. However, since English Auction is an open auction, as each buyer drops out of the auction, the remaining bidders can take these into account and revise their bidding strategies. If a buyer drops out, then that means that the current price has reached his maximum willingness to pay. From this the remaining bidders will infer that the private information possessed by the bidder who dropped out no longer permits him to bid more than the current price. Since we already know v_i is non-decreasing in X_j where $i \neq j$, the remaining bidders will not increase their valuations after a bidder drops out.

Affiliation

As already discussed in Chapter 3, when the valuations of buyers are correlated to one another rather than being independently distributed, we are in the world of affiliated valuations. Here, the valuation of one bidder depends not only on his own private information but also on the private information of all the other bidders.

The symmetric model

Let $X = \{X_1,..., X_N\}$. We assume that the signals X_i are drawn from the same interval $[0,\omega]$. For all i, $vi = u(X_i, X_{-i})$, where $X_{-i} = \{X_{i-1},... X_{i+1},..., X_N\}$ and the function $u(\cdot)$, which is the same for all the bidders, is symmetric in the last $N - 1$ components and $u(0) = 0$. This implies that only the set of private information of all the buyers matters; which buyer has what private information does not affect the valuation of any buyer. That is, the buyers are not important; the private information is the only determining factor for the construction of the valuations.

Define the function $v(x,y) = E(V_i|X_i = x, Y_1 = y)$ to be the expectation of the value to bidder i when the signal he receives is x, and the highest signal among the other bidders, Y_1, is y. Because of symmetry, this function is the same for all bidders, and v is a non-decreasing function of y. We assume that v is strictly increasing in x. Moreover, since $u(0) = 0$, we have $v(0,0) = 0$.

Second price sealed bid auction

Note that since bidders are not sure about their own valuations, they must bid according to the private information they have and the expected private information that the other bidders may have. The symmetric equilibrium in the second price sealed bid auction is given in Result 9.

Result 9: *Symmetric equilibrium strategies in a second price sealed bid auction are given by* $b(x) = v(x, x)$.

Note that b is increasing in x and that it can be shown that the equilibrium is unique in the class of symmetric equilibria with an increasing strategy.

First price sealed bid auction

The equilibrium bidding strategy for the first price sealed bid auction is complex. However, it is clear that no buyer will bid more than her valuation. Also, if b is the equilibrium bidding function, then $b(0) = 0$.

Result 10: *Symmetric equilibrium strategies in a first price sealed bid auction are given by* $b(x) = \int_0^x v(y,y)dL(y\,|\,x)$ *where* $L(y\,|\,x) = \exp\left(-\int_y^x \frac{g(t\,|\,t)}{G(t\,|\,t)}dt\right)$.

Note that here also b is increasing in x.

Revenue equivalence and efficiency consideration

If the seller is concerned about the expected revenue that an auction generates then under interdependent valuation with affiliated signals the seller should prefer second price sealed bid auction over first price sealed bid auction.

> **Result 11:** *The expected revenue from a second price sealed bid auction is at least as great as the expected revenue from a first price sealed bid auction when bidders have interdependent valuations in a symmetric framework.*

In fact, the seller may expect more revenue from the English Auction than from the second price sealed bid auction.

> **Result 12:** *The expected revenue from an English Auction is at least as great as the expected revenue from a second price sealed bid auction when bidders have interdependent valuations in a symmetric framework.*

The equilibrium strategies of first and second price sealed bid auctions, we have shown, are insulated from the winner's curse, as it can be shown that the bids are less than the expected value conditional on winning.

Here, as stated earlier, buyers do not know their valuations and only know their private information (signals). Since both first and second price sealed bid auctions have increasing bidding strategies that depend on private signals and not valuations, both the auctions will allocate the object to the buyer who has the highest signals and not the highest valuation. And the bidder with the highest signal need not be the one with the highest value. Recall that an auction is efficient if the bidder with the highest value is awarded the object. So in the case of interdependent valuations with affiliated signals, both the first and second price sealed bid auctions are inefficient.

However, if one additional condition is satisfied, then both auction formats become efficient. The condition is the famous *single crossing condition*.

The valuations satisfy the single crossing condition if for all i and $j \neq i$ and for all x, we have $\dfrac{\partial v_i}{\partial x_i}(x) \geq \dfrac{\partial v_j}{\partial x_i}(x)$.

> **Result 13:** *With symmetric, interdependent values and affiliated signals, suppose the single crossing condition is satisfied. Then second price and first price sealed bid auctions all have symmetric equilibria that are efficient.*

Multiple object auctions

Three types of sealed bid auctions

Although one can auction multiple objects in many ways, we will discuss three such ways here since these are the most standard ones. They are *discriminatory*, or *pay-your-bid auction, Uniform Price Auction* and *Vickrey Auction*. The first two auctions were widely used in many multiple object auctions in real life; however, the last one has many interesting theoretical properties that help devising policies regarding auction formats. We assume that the marginal values are falling, that is, one additional unit will give less utility than the previous unit. So if a buyer is bidding b_k for the kth unit and b_{k+1} for the $(k + 1)$th unit, then $b_k \geq b_{k+1}$ must hold. Suppose K identical objects are up for sell. The buyers are required to bid on each of them. So the bid of buyer i is a vector $b^i = \left(b_1^i \cdots, b_K^i \right)$, where $b_1^i \geq \cdots \geq b_K^i$ holds. Now we describe the three auction formats.

Discriminatory auction

In a discriminatory auction, every bidder makes payments of amounts equal to the sum of his bids that are deemed to be winning – that is, the sum of his bids that are among the K highest of the $N \times K$ bids submitted in all. For example, if buyer i wins four units of the object, then he must pay $b_1^i + b_2^i + b_3^i + b_4^i$. This type of auction is also known as *pay-your-bid* auction.

The discriminatory auction is not efficient; worse still, every equilibrium of the discriminatory auction is inefficient. A discriminatory auction can lead to efficient allocation only when the bidders have demand for just a single unit.

Uniform Price Auction

As the name suggests, in Uniform Price Auctions, all the winning bidders pay the same amount per unit of the object. The price must equate the demand and the supply of the objects. Thus the price must clear the market. All prices lying between the highest losing bid and the lowest winning bid are capable of equating the demand and the supply. Generally, the convention is to set the highest losing bid as the price per unit. So we assume here that the market clearing price is the same as the highest losing bid. Note that here all the winners pay the same amount to the seller.

Uniform price auctions may or may not be efficient. If a buyer wants more than one unit of the object, then the Uniform Price Auction may be inefficient. However, if a buyer wants only a single unit of the object, then Uniform Price Auction is efficient.

Vickrey Auction

In Vickrey Auction if a buyer wins k units of the object, then she has to pay the k highest competing losing bids, meaning that no bidder pays any bid that she quotes. As in the second price sealed bid auction, here it is always optimal for a buyer to report her true valuation for each unit of the objects.

> **Result 14:** *In a Vickrey Auction, the equilibrium bidding strategy is given by* $b(v) = v.$

So it is obvious that Vickrey Auction allocates the objects efficiently. We may note here that when there is single unit demand, then the Uniform Price Auction and the Vickrey Auction are one and the same. This follows straight from the payment rules. In the Uniform Price Auction with single unit demand, every bidder pays the highest losing bid, and in the case of the Vickrey Auction with single unit demand, every bidder pays the highest competing bid, and since every bidder demands only a single unit, everyone ends up paying the same highest losing bid. Thus, in case of single unit demand, Uniform Price Auctions turn into Vickrey Auctions and therefore allocate the objects efficiently. The intuition behind this phenomenon is that, when the bidders have demand for multiple units, in case of Uniform Price Auctions, the bid on the first unit decides whether the concerned bidder will win a unit or not, while any one of the bids on the second unit onwards might very well be the highest losing bid and thus the payment to be made by the concerned bidder. Every bidder tries to minimise this expected payment and thus suppresses the bid from the second unit onwards. In case of single unit demand, the payment to be made by any bidder is not dependent on her quoted bid, and therefore no bidder has any incentive to underbid, and so the allocation is based solely on the true valuations of the bidders ensuring efficiency. When bidders are symmetric, then even discriminatory auctions ensure efficient allocation for the case of single unit demand.[14] It is important to note here that at equilibrium, all the multiple unit auction formats yield the same expected revenue. Therefore, we have the following result.

> **Result 15:** *Under SIPV assumptions involving risk-neutral bidders, the Revenue Equivalence Principle holds for multiple unit auctions.*

Two types of open bid auctions

Dutch Auction

The multi-unit Dutch (open descending price) Auction is very similar to the single unit case. Here the auctioneer begins by announcing a very high price of an object. The buyers should indicate how many units they want at that price. Since the price is very high, usually no buyer wants to buy any units of the object. Then the auctioneer lowers the price. If at that price at least one buyer wants to buy at least one unit of the object, she gets the units she demands at that price. Then the auctioneer again lowers the price, and the auction continues until all the units are sold. The examples stated earlier in this chapter establish the fact that Dutch Auctions are more commonly used for multiple objects as opposed to single objects.

English Auction

The multi-unit English (open descending price) auction (like the multi-unit Dutch Auction) is very similar to its single unit counterpart. Here the auctioneer begins by announcing a very low price of a single unit of object. The buyers should indicate how many units they want at that price. Since the price is very low, usually there is more demand for the object than the supply. Then the auctioneer gradually increases the price until demand matches the supply. All the units are sold at the price where demand is equal to the supply.

Package auctions

In case of sale of multiple objects, one important consideration is that relating to synergy. When the valuation derived from having a number of objects together exceeds the sum of the individual valuations for the respective objects, positive synergy is said to be present. Similarly, when the valuation for the objects being possessed together falls short of the sum of the individual values, negative synergy is said to be present. Positive and negative synergies are also alternatively termed as *super-additive* and *sub-additive* values, respectively. For example, if there are two objects, a bidder assigns individual values V_1 and V_2, respectively, to them, and the total valuation for having the objects together is V, then positive synergy is present when $V > V_1 + V_2$, while negative synergy is present when $V < V_1 + V_2$. This aspect of synergies can be observed in real-life auctions of licenses for telecom spectrum. It might be quite possible that possessing two particular telecom circles generates super-additive value for the operator due to certain interdependencies or cost advantages. Similarly, when two telecom circles are more or less alike i.e., have the characteristics of a substitute, then possessing them together may result in sub-additive values for the operator.

In presence of positive synergies, package auctions – i.e., bundling the objects together for which the super-additive value works – improves the revenue prospect, while for negative synergies, selling the objects separately leads to the generation of higher expected revenue. For positive synergies, if the objects are sold separately, a bidder who has super-additive valuation is likely to bid a lower amount on the first unit since there is no certainty of obtaining the second unit, and in case the second unit is not won by the concerned bidder, he will incur losses. This induces lower bidding in the auction process, which somewhat depresses the revenue prospects. This can be understood easily since for positive synergy, $V - V_2 > V_1$. Therefore, if a bidder is uncertain about the prospect of winning the second item, he will bid V_1 for the first unit and V_2 for the second unit in a second price sealed bid auction. However, if the two items are offered as a package, then the concerned bidder will bid V in a second price sealed bid auction. This particular problem is known as the *exposure problem*. The exposure problem can be mitigated by package auctions.

Thus depending on the context, the auction designers have to very carefully select the mode of auction so that the intended objectives are fulfilled in the best possible manner. How auction designing in real life can prove challenging can be best understood by looking at actual experiences. Chapters 5 and 6 elaborate experiences on real-life auctions.

Notes

1 The distinction between independent and interdependent valuations has been elaborated in detail in Chapter 3.
2 https://en.wikipedia.org/wiki/Dutch_auction
3 https://en.wikipedia.org/wiki/Aalsmeer_Flower_Auction
4 https://corporatefinanceinstitute.com/resources/knowledge/finance/dutch-auction/
5 https://corporatefinanceinstitute.com/resources/knowledge/deals/ipo-initial-public-offering/
6 The mathematical expressions used in this section are mostly taken from Krishna (2010).
7 The distinction between risk-neutral and risk-averse bidders has been elaborated in Chapter 3.
8 The distinction between risk-neutral and risk-averse bidders has been elaborated in Chapter 3.
9 This equivalence is entirely in the ex-ante sense; the ex-post materialised revenue may very well vary.
10 This holds true when we assume away possibilities of collusion among bidders.
11 The case of risk-averse bidders has been discussed in Chapter 3.
12 http://citeseerx.ist.psu.edu/viewdoc/download?doi=10.1.1.152.9865&rep=rep1&type=pdf
13 The notions of asymmetric bidding have been elaborated in Chapter 3.
14 The proof of this claim is a bit technical and thus forgone here. Interested readers may look up Krishna (2010, p. 200).

5 Auctions

Some real-life experiences

Introduction

Auctions have been in use worldwide since antiquity for the allocation of a varied range of objects. As noted earlier in this book, even the Roman Empire was auctioned in 193 C.E. To date, auction as an allocation mechanism remains quite popular across countries. Auction is being adopted as the method of allocation for many new objects. Many countries that used other methods of allocation for certain objects like spectrum licenses, mining rights etc. are increasingly switching to auctions (Jilani 2015). In a majority of countries these days, auction is the chosen method for the allocation of radio spectrum, e.g., the United States, the UK, Australia, New Zealand, Germany, Turkey and India. Auction as an allocation mechanism is not just becoming increasingly adopted for the allocation of radio spectrum licenses, it is a chosen mechanism for the allocation of a multitude of other types of goods. The examples range from a variety of antiques; collectibles such as stamps, coins, vintage toys and trains; classic cars; fine art; luxury real estate; wine, fish, wool, timber etc. In many countries across the world second-hand goods are also put up for sale through auction. Online auctions for the sale of second-hand goods are rapidly gaining popularity, as is shown by the growth of e-auctions through websites like eBay or Snapdeal. Among other things, the auction of emission permits is very important. Governments of countries provide rights to industrial houses to emit polluting gases, like CO_2, NO_2 etc., within limits through licenses, and these licenses are allotted through auctions. The examples of such auctions of emission permits by governments are visible in the United States, Australia, the EU and elsewhere.

Since the auction of telecom spectrum licenses is the most common auction across the world, this chapter discusses telecom spectrum auction in one section, followed by a discussion of certain unforeseen problems that have cropped up in telecom spectrum auctions.

Radio spectrum auction: some countries' experiences

A large number of countries all over the world are using auctions for allocating telecom spectrum licenses. This section discusses the early telecom spectrum license auctions for the United States of America (U.S.), the United Kingdom (UK) and the Netherlands. The United States has been very successful in running auctions and allocating spectrum licenses. The very first telecom spectrum auction conducted by the UK created history and came to be known as the "biggest auction ever". Despite using the same auction design, the Netherlands spectrum auction is usually regarded as a blunder. This section presents an analytical comparative discussion to identify the subtle issues to keep in mind while designing auctions in terms of the country experiences.

United States of America (U.S.)

In the United States, the Federal Communications Commission (FCC), established in 1934, is in charge of allocating electromagnetic spectrum licenses. For the allocation of these licenses, the FCC has been conducting auctions since 1994. So far, ninety such auctions have been conducted, and revenue worth tens of billions of dollars has been generated for the U.S. Treasury. So various countries across the world are taking lessons from the auction designs of the FCC. An important feature of the FCC auction is that the FCC always selects the spectrum reclaimed from other uses for auction. A few examples include the spectrum returned by television broadcasters after the digital television transition and the spectrum made available by federal agencies able to shift their operations to other bands. The FCC sets eligibility criteria, and whichever company or individual qualifies according to these criteria can take part in the auctions. Every participant has to make an upfront refundable payment towards the bids they plan to submit in the auction. A bidder's maximum bidding eligibility, which is the maximum amount of bidding units on which the applicant will be permitted to bid in any single round of bidding, is defined by the number of bidding units purchased with this upfront payment.

Since its establishment in 1934, the FCC has allotted spectrum licenses using other allocation mechanisms like Comparative Hearings or lotteries. The Commission primarily relied on these mechanisms to select a single licensee from a pool of mutually exclusive applicants for a license. However, eventually the FCC came to realise that auction as a method of electromagnetic spectrum allocation is much more efficient compared to other methods. The U.S. Congress in 1993 passed the Omnibus Budget Reconciliation Act. This Act assigned the authority to the FCC for using competitive bidding for selection from among two or more mutually exclusive applications for an initial license. Auction as an allocation mechanism for the allotment of licenses was adopted with the objective of assigning the licenses to those who can use them in the best possible manner. Moreover, the usage of auctions has led to substantial reductions in the average time from initial application to the granting of license to less than one year. Also, the financial benefit from the award of licenses is reaching the public directly now.

When spectrum auction was first launched, multiple goals were set for FCC by the U.S. Congress:

> *In designing auctions for spectrum licenses, the FCC is required by law to meet multiple goals and not focus simply on maximizing receipts. Those goals include ensuring efficient use of the spectrum, promoting economic opportunity and competition, avoiding excessive concentration of licenses, preventing the unjust enrichment of any party, and fostering the rapid deployment of new services, as well as recovering for the public a portion of the value of the spectrum.*[1]

The auction design followed by the FCC was simultaneous multiple-round (SMR) type. These auctions are conducted electronically and are accessible through the Internet. Anyone using a personal computer with an Internet connection and a browser can access the FCC Automated Auction System. The term *simultaneous* in SMR auctions is explained by the fact that each license is available for bidding throughout the entire auction. These types of auctions, contrasted to many other formats involving a continuum of bids, have discrete rounds in a sequence, with the length of each round announced in advance by the Commission. At the closing of each round, the results for the concerned round are processed and made available for public viewing. Round results are disclosed within approximately 15 minutes after the closing of each round. Only at this point of time do bidders get to observe the bids placed by other contending bidders. The results can be downloaded by both the bidders and the general public. Interested parties may perform detailed analysis by loading these data files into a spreadsheet program or the Auction Tracking Tool, which is provided by the FCC for most auctions.

This information signals the value of the licenses to other contending bidders. It also increases the likelihood that the licenses will be assigned to the bidders who value them the most. The interval between two consecutive auction rounds provides the scope to bidders for taking stock of, as well as adjusting their bidding strategies. The number of rounds in any SMR auction cannot be predetermined. It is totally contingent on how long the bidders stay active. Thus, bidding continues in a sequence of rounds until a round occurs in which all bidder activity ceases, and this round is considered to be the closing round of the auction.

The auction design, the number of bidders, and the number of licenses being offered become decisive for how long an auction will run. The duration may vary from one day to several weeks. The auctions held by FCC are typically conducted during normal business hours (Eastern Time) from Monday to Friday. On the first day, an auction generally opens with long bidding periods, typically two bidding rounds each with duration of one or two hours, followed by round results. During the auction, the number of rounds per day is generally increased by the Commission, combined with a decrease in the duration of the rounds. Bidders continue to drop out of the auction when the prices of the licenses in which they are interested exceed their willingness to pay. The auction stops when all bidding activity stops.

Bidders, in a traditional real-time or continuous auction, quite often hold their bids initially and wait until the last minute to place them. To check this possibility, the FCC has designed activity rules to ensure active bidding by the participants throughout the auction. As noted earlier in this section, each bidder has to make an upfront payment prior to an auction that determines its bidding eligibility in the auction. Every bidder is required to bid on a specified portion of its maximum eligibility during each round of the auction. If a bidder fails to meet this requirement, it uses an activity rule waiver (if available) or loses eligibility.

The FCC issues a public notice declaring an auction concluded at the closing of the auction. This notice identifies winning bidders and specifies the amounts of down payments due. The winning bidders are typically allowed ten business days to supplement their upfront payments to satisfy the license down payment requirement. Also within this deadline, the winning bidders have to electronically submit a properly completed long-form application and required exhibits to the appropriate licensing bureau.

Authorised by Congress in 2012, the FCC commenced the first ever so-called incentive auction on March 29, 2016. This auction was designed to repurpose spectrum for new uses, using market forces to align the use of broadcast airwaves with twenty-first-century consumer demands for video and broadband services. The auction was concluded on March 30, 2017, "repurposing 84 megahertz of spectrum – 70 megahertz for licensed use and another 14 megahertz for wireless microphones and unlicensed use". The auction generated $19.8 billion in revenue, including $10.05 billion for winning broadcast bidders and more than $7 billion to be deposited to the U.S. Treasury for deficit reduction.[2]

The incentive auction preserves a robust broadcast TV industry but at the same time enables stations to generate additional revenues that they can invest into programming and services to the communities they serve. The incentive auction ensures the availability of valuable low-band airwaves for wireless broadband, and consumers are likely to benefit from the incentive auction due to the easing of congestion on wireless networks. The incentive auction is also laying the foundation for fifth-generation (5G) wireless services and applications, as well as stimulating job creation and economic growth.

United Kingdom (UK)

In the United Kingdom, the Office of Communications, commonly known as Ofcom, is the government-approved authority in charge of regulatory functions and competition. Ofcom's creation was announced in 2001, in the Queen's speech to the UK Parliament. Ofcom was preceded by the Broadcasting Standards Commission, the Independent Television Commission, the Office of Telecommunications (Oftel), the Radio Authority, and the Radiocommunications Agency, respectively, which performed the same functions.

The first spectrum auction in the UK was conducted during March 6 to April 27, 2000 by the Radiocommunications Agency. This auction involved one hundred fifty rounds. Thirteen bidders contested for the five licenses during the seven weeks of bidding. The bidding began in phase 2 since all conflicts with associated bidders were resolved prior to qualification. The government's overall aim for the auction was "to secure, for the long term benefit of United Kingdom customers and the national economy, the timely and economically advantageous development and sustained provision of third-generation services in the United Kingdom". Keeping these aims in mind, the government worked with the following objectives:

- Utilise the available spectrum with optimum efficiency
- Promote effective and sustainable competition for the provision of third-generation services
- Subject to the overall objectives, design an auction that is judged to best realise the full economic value to customers, industry and the taxpayer of the spectrum

The first auction yielded a revenue amounting to £22.5 billion (US$34 billion) for five third-generation (3G) mobile wireless licenses. Although the UK resorted to auction for the allocation of spectrum licenses as late as 2000, the first auction itself emerged as a huge success story. In fact, this very first auction came to be known as the world's "biggest ever" auction.

A simultaneous ascending auction was used for allocating five 3G licenses, A–E. All licenses have a twenty-year duration. The bandwidth for each license is shown in Table 5.1.

The licenses from B to E were available for bidding by all bidders, while license A was kept reserved for new entrants. Thus only potential new entrants were eligible to bid on this license.

The simultaneous ascending auction format used in the UK was a variant of the SMR design used in the United States. The UK design had an inherent advantage in terms of the simple license structure. Being geographically a much smaller country compared to United States, the UK could afford to design an auction for which each bidder could win at most one license. The United States, on the other hand, has many regions, and most of the U.S. auctions involved many licenses within each region. This fact largely complicated the bidding strategy.

In the UK auction, all five licenses were offered for sale simultaneously. The auction proceeded through a succession of rounds. In every round, bidders who were "not the current price bidder on a license could place a bid on a license, raising the price on that license by at least the minimum bid increment". At the closing of the round, "all bids and bidders were identified, together with the price bid (highest bid) and bidder for each license and the minimum bid in the next round". The auction stopped at the point where no bidder expressed willingness to bid higher on any of the licenses. This format bears resemblance to the well known English Auction for the sale of multiple units with interdependent values.

The prices far surpassed the expectations of all: the government, the industry, the bidders and also the taxpayers. The auction was successful in generating revenues beyond all expectations. The amount of revenue generated in the UK 3G auction exceeded the total revenues of all U.S. spectrum auctions conducted over the prior six years. This is quite remarkable since the United States is 4.5 times the size of the UK. The total amounts to 650 euros per person or 1,100 euros per current subscriber.

The majority of the bidders adopted the strategy of bidding on the license that represented the best value. Thus switching from license to license with

Table 5.1 Bandwidth in MHz for each license

	A	B	C	D	E
Paired spectrum	2 × 15	2 × 15	2 × 10	2 × 10	2 × 10
Unpaired spectrum	5	0	5	5	5
Total	35	30	25	25	25

Source: www.cramton.umd.edu/papers2000-2004/01nao-cramton-report-on-uk-3g-auction.pdf

price changes by bidders was observed. Only Vodafone and Orange were exceptions. Both of them staked out particular markets. Vodafone had bid exclusively on the B license, the only large license available to incumbents, at times resorting to jump bids (i.e., bids above the minimum bid) to indicate its resolve to win the B license. Even the final bid by Vodafone was a jump bid. Orange consistently pursued the E license, bidding exclusively on E, once the B license became too expensive. The summary of results is shown in Table 5.2.

The understanding of the existing market structure and how the auction works make it possible to identify a predictable pattern in the pricing dynamics, though the absolute level of prices could not be predicted so accurately. First, there were four incumbents: Vodafone, BT, Orange and One2One. Potential entrants definitely have much lower values compared to incumbents. For an incumbent, the value of a license consists of the value of future 3G services plus the value of 2G revenues lost if it fails to secure a license, while for an entrant, the value of a license is simply the value of future 3G services less the cost of building a network. An incumbent's existing infrastructure reduces its 3G build-out cost. It can be reasonably expected that consumers would prefer to have 2G services from an operator who has plans for 3G service. Finally, the more 2G customers an operator has, the easier it is to attract 3G customers. Therefore, it can be easily predicted that each of the four incumbents would win a license and that the A license would land up in the hands of the strongest new entrant. Vodafone or BT being the strongest among the incumbents financially and also likely to have the highest value for 3G services owing to their much larger market shares compared to the younger incumbents, the second largest license would end up with either of these two. The only uncertainties were about (1) identifying the strongest potential entrant and (2) the relative strength of Vodafone and BT vis-à-vis each other.

Two bidders effectively became decisive for all the prices: (1) BT, the strongest among the three incumbents that failed to win a large license, and

Table 5.2 Auction winners and winning bids

	A	B	C	D	E
MHz paired	2 × 15	2 × 15	2 × 10	2 × 10	2 × 10
MHz unpaired	5	0	5	5	5
Bidder	T/W	Vodafone	BT	121	Orange
Price bid (£M)	4,385	5,964	4,030	4,004	4,095
£M/MHz paired	292	398	403	400	410

Source: www.cramton.umd.edu/papers2000-2004/01nao-cramton-report-on-uk-3g-auction.pdf

(2) NTL, the strongest among the eight unsuccessful new entrants. NTL dropped out of the auction in round 148, but by that time it had effectively set the price for C, D, E at just over £4 billion. NTL's arbitrage between the large A license and the smaller C, D and E licenses had also set TIW's price for the A license. That the new entrants did not value the extra 5 MHz of paired spectrum very much was evident from the bidding of NTL and the other new entrants. The two largest incumbents, on the other hand, attached great value to the extra 5 MHz. By placing its final bid on the B license in round 142, BT effectively set the price for that license. Vodafone's price per MHz roughly equaled the prices paid for the small incumbent licenses (C, D and E).

The decision of auctioning five licenses had a serious impact on revenues since it ensured the winning of at least one license for the new entrants. The certainty of winning generated a strong incentive for potential entrants, especially the strong ones, to take part in the bidding process. This incentive to participate was further strengthened by the critical choice of setting aside the largest license for a new entrant. The whole design not only guaranteed the winning of a new entrant, but it also ensured that the best license would be won by the successful entrant.

Two more factors related to the timing of the auction played a decisive role in generating the high revenues. First, in the sequence of European 3G auctions, the UK auction was the first. It was believed by the largest wireless operators that an important first step in becoming or sustaining a major position in Europe was to win a license in the UK. Thus the UK was perceived to be the threshold that needed to be crossed to gain entry through the door to Europe and potentially the world. In general, for a sequence of auctions where the items have complementarity or superadditive values, winning the items sold earlier generates a competitive advantage for the winning bidders in the subsequent auctions, and thus the early items always sell at higher prices. Another factor that also contributed to the high amount of revenue generation was that, this being the first auction, the bidders lacked enough experience to predict the extremely high prices that would result if they did not form alliances prior to the auction.

Second, the auction took place when the high-technology stock bubble was apparently at its peak, when the values of wireless and other high-tech companies were running at all-time highs and at unheard of price-earnings multiples. The failure to win a license did not merely mean a loss of value; rather, this question of value transformed into a question of how much a company would suffer in terms of its stock price due to its failure to win a license. This concern plagued not only the incumbents but also the strongest new entrants. The payment of four billion pounds for entry into the 3G business seemed reasonable with UK wireless companies being valued in the tens of billions. Thus inflated stock market values bore a direct impact on the companies' willingness to bid.

The obvious impact was a substantial loss of stock market confidence, due to which the ratio of debt to assets based on share price changed, making the telephone operators' effective credit rating look insecure. The telecom developers were now in a fix. They had invested heavily in research and development over the years in order to maintain parity with changing technology. The telecom operators were no longer in a position to pay even the maintenance and upgrading charges on the ordinary landline equipment, let alone buy something new. Europe witnessed 100,000 job losses in the support and development industry within a year, the UK alone being responsible for 30,000 of these.

Paul Klemperer, the eminent faculty member of Economics at Oxford University as well as adviser to the UK government in its 3G auction, has disputed whether the crash should be blamed on the auction rather than on broader economic problems. He partly agrees that the bidders had mistakenly quoted very high bids on the licenses and that the money was a transfer from shareholders to the governments, but at the same time he argues that the one-off and upfront sunk costs of the auction should have had no effect when considering the profitability of future investment and should not have significantly affected the future behaviour of the telecoms companies. He also notes that in the UK it was NTL (which failed in its bid) that ended up in the most miserable financial situation and raises the question whether the $100 billion cost of the auctions could explain the $700 billion drop in two years that was observed in the market capitalisation of the telecoms companies.[3]

The Netherlands

In Europe, the Netherlands introduced second-generation (2G) mobile telephony quite late. The Dutch government in March 1995 distributed two licenses to operate 2G networks using frequencies in the 900-MHz band. The incumbent monopolist, KPN, obtained one license, and the second one was won by Libertel, a joint venture of Vodafone and ING-Bank at that time, through a Beauty Contest. At the same time, the Dutch government felt the necessity to quickly provide licenses to additional mobile operators using spectrum in the 1,800-MHz band. The Dutch government also felt it was desirable to allot such additional licenses through auction. Therefore in July 1995, the government decided to choose auction as the preferred mechanism. Considerable time had elapsed since the telecommunication law required to be changed to award licenses through auctions rather than by means of Beauty Contests, and therefore it was only in February 1998 that the DCS-1800 auction actually took place.

In the Dutch DCS-1800 auction, spectrum in the 1,800-MHz band was sold by using a variant of the simultaneous multiple round ascending auction. It is important to note for our discussion that the number of licenses offered in this auction was endogenous and that the auction produced three winners. Dutchtone and Telfort won the two large lots (of 15 MHz each) and Ben acquired 16.8 MHz of spectrum through the purchase of several smaller lots in the auction and also by buying spectrum from losing parties after the auction. Thus the Netherlands had five 2G operators, while other European countries typically had either three or four of them.

The Netherlands was the second European country to auction Universal Mobile Telecommunications Service (UMTS) licenses, and this auction closely followed the so-called biggest auction ever in the UK. This auction involved 306 rounds of bidding during July 6 to July 24, 2000. The Dutch government had the following objectives:

- Efficiently allocate the available spectrum
- Contribute towards having a competitive telecommunications market

It must be noted here that the 2G licenses were distributed in the spring of 1998. Thus, at the time of the 3G auction, these DCS-1800 operators had only two years of market experience, and they were in a certain sense relative newcomers. Their market shares also reflected this. In the summer of 2000, KPN had 49 per cent of the subscribers, Libertel 31 per cent, Telfort 7.3 per cent, Dutchtone 6.9 per cent and Ben 5.8 per cent.

Immediately after the 2G auction, the Dutch government started preparing for the 3G auction. On July 16, 1998, a consultation document was published, and discussion with market parties was conducted later that year. A policy proposal emerged as a result of these discussions that was published on March 25, 1999. In line with the recommendation of the UMTS Forum,[4] four licenses, each lasting for fifteen years and consisting of 2 × 15 MHz of paired spectrum and 5 MHz of unpaired spectrum, were planned for allocation. Incumbents (i.e., existing 2G operators) were not to be barred from taking part in the auction, no license was to be reserved for potential entrants, and no fresh entrant was to receive special roaming rights on existing 2G networks.

The auction rules were published in April 2000. The following aspects of the rules are relevant in this context:

- Five licenses were auctioned. Licenses A and B involved 2 × 15 MHz of paired spectrum and 1 × 5 MHz of unpaired spectrum. Each of the licenses C, D, E involved 2 × 10 MHz of paired spectrum and 1 × 5 MHz of unpaired. The license duration was fifteen years.

- The licenses were sold in a simultaneous multiple round auction.
- Each bidder could bid on each license; however, in each round, one could bid on at most one license, and if one was standing high on some lot, for example lot L one was not allowed to bid on a different lot; hence each bidder could acquire at most one license.
- In the first round, the minimum required bid on lots A and B was ƒ100 million; it was ƒ90 million on lots C, D, E. If there was no bid on a lot, the minimum price for the next round was reduced to 70 (resp. 60), and if there was no bid in the next rounds, the minimum was further reduced to 35 and next to 0 (resp. 30 and 0).
- Each bidder had three waivers (or pass cards); waivers could be used in only one of the first 30 rounds of the auction.
- A bidder who was not standing high on a lot and who was not bidding, or not using a waiver, was no longer eligible to bid.
- Bidders knew who was standing high on each lot.
- For each lot, the auctioneer determined the minimum bid that was relevant for the next round; the bid increment was at most 10 per cent of the previous highest bid on the lot, or 200,000 guilders if the latter amount was higher.
- Bidders were not allowed to disturb the proper course of the auction; they were not allowed to prevent competition from taking place in the auction.
- The auction ended when no more bids were made, with parties having the highest bids at that time winning the licenses; the winners had to pay their final bids.

In the morning of July 6, the day on which the auction started, the Dutch government was surprised to discover only six bidders, e.g., KPN, Libertel, Ben, Dutchtone, Telfort and Versatel. But it was too late to call off the auction. During the thirteen-day duration of the auction, there were 305 bidding rounds, and when in round 306 Versatel decided not to bid, the auction ended. The auction was, for the most part, uneventful, and it fetched less than 3 billion euros as opposed to the almost 10 billion euros predicted by the Dutch government based on the UK experience.[5]

Thus the Dutch Auction was a major flop, in stark contrast to the highly successful UK auction. Two days after the completion of the Dutch Auction, in an opinion piece in the *Financial Times*, Paul Klemperer called the Dutch Auction a failure and posed the question:

So why did the Netherlands' auction, using similar bidding rules to the UK one, attract so few competitors and such feeble bidding, and raise barely a quarter of the per capita revenue of the UK auction?

(Klemperer, 2000)

According to Klemperer, the Dutch Auction had gone wrong on two counts. First and foremost, they chose the wrong auction design. In a market with five incumbent 2G operators, five 3G licenses should not have been offered in a simultaneous multiple round ascending auction since, as an auction, it provides newcomers little scope for winning a license. Some alternative auction format, for example the "Anglo-Dutch" design, would have been more favourable for newcomers, and therefore it could have encouraged more auction participation and more aggressive bidding, leading to higher revenues generation for the Dutch government. Second, the Dutch government should have devised a tougher competition policy in order to prevent competitors from forming alliances with one another prior to the auction.

However, to assess the performance of the Dutch spectrum auction objectively, it must be noted that all these criticisms seem valid, but the basis of judgment should be whether it achieved the desired goals. The originally pronounced goals of the Dutch government were neither attracting many bidders, nor establishing new market entry, nor obtaining high revenue. The appropriateness of these goals can definitely be questioned, and it may be argued that revenue maximisation and generating entry should have been explicit goals. Be that as it may, in retrospect, in terms of revenue, the Dutch government did not do so badly after all.

Some other countries' experiences in spectrum auction and the lessons from them

As noted in earlier chapters, collusion among bidders can seriously depress revenue generation in auctions. The spectrum auction experience in New Zealand is a glaring example of that. The New Zealand government in 1990 conducted the auction of radio spectrum for the first time. The New Zealand government had sought advice from NERA, a consultancy firm and adopted the second price sealed bid format[6] for the auction of the first four licenses. The licenses to deliver television signals were essentially identical, and a simultaneous second price sealed tender auction was conducted for each license. As noted by McMillan (1994), "In one extreme case, a firm that had bid NZ$100,000 paid the second-highest bid of NZ$6. In another the high bid was NZ$7 million and the second bid was NZ$5,000." Thus the actual revenue generation was just NZ$36 million as opposed to NZ$250 million as predicted by the consultants.[7] The New Zealand government immediately switched to the *first price sealed bid* format. However, the problem still could not be fully resolved.

According to Milgrom (2004), alternative auction formats could probably have performed better in New Zealand: first, the Dutch flower auction, where the winner in the first round is allowed to take as many lots as it intends at the winning price and, once that is done, has the right to choose the next licence to be sold in the next auction round, could have been adopted since this format prevents bidders from guessing about which licenses to bid on; second, the New Zealand government could have also followed the United States online auction formats, which allows bidders to specify both price and quantity and for which the highest bidders get their ordered quantities in full "with only the last winning bidder running the risk of having to settle for a partial order". Another alternative policy option that can be considered for meeting a revenue target hinges on the issue of reserve prices. If the government can identify a suitable reserve price that is the minimum price that any winning bidder must pay, then the loss of revenue can be mitigated to a large extent.

How designing an auction may even lead to non-allocation of resources is observed in the case of Turkey's spectrum auction.[8] Turkey, in the year 2000, auctioned two telecom spectrum licenses in sequence. The Turkey government had set the reserve price of the second license equal to the selling price of the first one. One firm chose to bid an amount much higher than the actual worth on the first license when two firms were to operate in the market with the other firm holding the second license. The firm that submitted a very high bid on the first license had strategically calculated that no firm would bid that high for the second license, and this strategic prediction indeed came out to be true. Thus the net outcome was that the second license remained unallocated, and the firm winning the first license effectively operated as a monopolist.

Conclusion

The discussion in the preceding sections provides empirical support to the theoretical discussion in Chapter 2 on the challenges of auction designing. Certain possibilities can be theoretically foreseen, and accordingly activity rules can be devised. However, in real life, so many other factors come into play leading to quite unexpected turns of events that the auction theorists are forced to undergo rethinking continuously on the designing issues. The theoretical aspects and empirical studies thus have a nice complementary role: while the empirical evidence helps auction theorists learn about new aspects in designing auctions, the theoretical understanding of auctions helps in assessing the observed phenomena and taking the right kind of lessons for future auction designs and devising appropriate activity rules from the observed experiences.

Notes

1 Rose, G. F., & Lloyd, M. (2006, May). *The failure of FCC spectrum auctions (PDF)*. Center for American Progress. Retrieved from https://cdn.americanpro gress.org/wp-content/uploads/kf/SPECTRUM_AUCTIONS_MAY06.PDF
2 www.fcc.gov/about-fcc/fcc-initiatives/incentive-auctions
3 www.paulklemperer.org/PressArticles/FT26Nov2002PDKAuctionsLb.pdf
4 Report number 5, September 1998 as quoted in van-Damme (2002).
5 Spectrum Auctions and Competition in Telecommunications, edited by Gerhard Illing and Ulrich Klüh (2003).
6 This format was originally described by Vickrey (1961), the rules of which have been elaborated earlier in this book.
7 Milgrom (2004).
8 This incident is referred to in Klemperer (2004).

6 Auctions in India

Introduction

It is a common practice worldwide to allocate natural resources, especially when scarce, through auction, and this practice is common in India as well. In India, two quite important natural resources are allocated through auction: telecom/radio spectrum licenses and mining rights in coal mines. Both these resources are publicly owned. Telecom spectra, also sometimes referred to as airwaves or frequencies, can definitely be considered to be in the category of scarce natural resources. Prior to 1995, telecom spectrum was believed to be a property of the government. But, in a case between the Cricket Association of Bengal and the Union of India, the Supreme Court in 1995 gave the verdict that "[t]he airwaves or frequencies are a public property. Their use has to be controlled and regulated by a public authority in the interests of the public and to prevent the invasion of their rights. Since, the electronic media involves the use of the airwaves, this factor creates an in-built restriction on its use as in the case of any other public property".[1] India started auctioning telecom spectrum licenses in 1991 and thus joined the club of the early adopters of auction in the allocation process of radio spectrum licenses in the world. After that, the telecom spectrum licenses have been allocated through auctions many times, e.g., in the years 1994, 1995, 1997, 2000, 2001, 2010, 2012, 2013, 2014, 2015, 2016 and 2017. Also, there are proposals for the of new generation technology telecom spectrum licenses in 2018.

Among the auctions conducted so far, some have been remarkably successful and some not so much. In this chapter, we will discuss these auctions with the objective of identifying and analysing their positive aspects or drawbacks from the viewpoint of Auction Theory. The next three sections discuss the telecom spectrum auctions conducted in India so far,[2] and the final discusses the coal auction.

Telecom spectrum auctions: 1991–2001

The first auction of spectrum licenses in India occurred in 1991. The auctions of spectrum licenses in India is conducted by the Department of Telecommunications (DoT). In the auction of 1991, based on the revenue potential, the entire country was divided into twenty circles, categorised as A, B and C for service provision. In order to ensure administrative convenience, the smaller states were clubbed together while the larger states were divided into more than one circle. For regular services, the DoT decided to have one additional operator along with the DoT per area, while for cellular services, there were two providers per area. The auction rules in 1991 required every potential service provider to have a foreign partner. The rationale guiding this rule was the feeling that Indian providers lacked adequate technical knowledge and financial resources. The first price sealed bid auction format was used. The Global System for Mobile Communications (GSM) was designated as India's accepted cellular technology by DoT. Preceding the auction, no specification was provided about the maximum number of licenses that could be awarded to an individual provider. After all the bids were collected, a single company was discovered to have won nine circles submitting very high bids. However, uncertainty prevailed regarding the prospects of the payment of license fees by this company as the payment requirements were $15 billion over fifteen years, whereas its annual turnover at that point was just $0.06 billion.[3] Also, one of GoI's major objectives was ensuring competition in the telecom sector. This objective would have been defeated had nine circles been awarded to a single company. So this company was offered to choose any three circles out of the nine won. Fifteen circles were offered for rebidding, for which the government specified reserve prices. However, the bidders perceived the reserve prices to be too high, resulting in very poor participation. The outcome was that nine of the circles remained unallocated to any provider.

In 1994 the GoI announced the National Telecom Policy of paving the way for private sector participation in the telecom industry. Private companies were invited to bid for basic and cellular licenses separately for each circle. DoT specified GSM for cellular services, and foreign partnership was also mandated in 1995. During that period, Code Division Multiple Access (CDMA)[4] mobile network started to be deployed in various parts of the world. In the first bidding round, the government invited bids for each circle for basic wireless services, but when the bids were opened in August 1995, Himachal Futuristics Communications Limited (HFCL) had the highest bid in nine circles. In many cases, its bid was more than double the second highest bid. At this point the government announced a cap of three circles for a single bidder in Category A and B circles, excluding Category C circles and extending the cap to cellular bids. Also, the GoI rejected the highest bids in ten telecom circles on the grounds that they were below the reserve price. The reserve price, however, had not been announced prior to the auction. An obvious consequence of such policies was multiple rounds of bidding. The government's decision to use the valuation of the bidders in each round of auction as an input for fixing the reserve price for the next round might have contributed to collusion among the bidders, leading to lower bids in order to force the government to reduce the reserve price.[5] Even though in 1995, the Indian government reduced reserve prices in order to attract bidders, the licenses in eight of the twenty-one circles still remained unallocated.

The bidders selected for each circle were asked to match the license fee quoted by the highest bidder. As a result of this process, 34 licenses were issued in 18 circles. The second bidding round also faced major problems. As more lucrative circles had been awarded in the first round, there was a lack of enthusiasm, and only six bids were received. Naturally initial service rollout was slow, as a result of narrow licensing conditions and the high cost of license fees.

The payment rules in the auctions conducted in 1994 and 1995 required the second highest bidders to match the winning bids. In many cases, the second highest bidders failed to do so as the difference between the highest and the second highest bids was very high.[6]

In 2008, 122 new second generation (2G) Unified Access Service (UAS) licenses were distributed on a First-Come-First-Served (FCFS) basis to telecom companies at 2001 prices. The Central Bureau of Investigation (CBI) filed a charge sheet indicating corruption in the distribution process. It was alleged that the distribution of licenses had been in favour of certain companies subject to payment of bribes by them and that some of these companies did not have prior experience in telecom operations.

Among the recent auctions, the 3G and 4G telecom spectrum were auctioned in highly competitive bidding in 2010. Tata Docomo was the first private operator to launch 3G services in India.[7] The government earned a total revenue of over Rs. 106219 crores (US\$19 billion) from the 3G and the broadband wireless auctions.[8] In 2012, the DoT auctioned 2G spectrum in both the GSM and the CDMA bands. The government received bids worth a total of Rs. 9,407 crores, far lower than its target of Rs. 28,000 crores from the sale of 2G spectrum in the GSM band. None of the bidders bid for a pan-India spectrum, for which the reserve price was set at Rs. 140 billion for 5 MHz of airwaves.[9] In March 2013, the DoT auctioned 2G spectrum in GSM (1,800-MHz) and CDMA (800-MHz) bands. Response to the 2013 spectrum auction was poor. While there were no bidders for spectrum in the 1,800-MHz and 900-MHz bands, Sistema Shyam Teleservices Ltd. (SSTL), which is also known as MTS India[10] (since it is the Indian subdivision of the

Russia-based Mobile Tele Systems [MTS] telecommunications company), was the only bidder for airwaves in the 800 MHz-band. Some companies complained about the very high reserve prices that, according to them, have deterred entry of many potential bidders.[11] 2G telecom spectrum licenses in the frequency range of 900 MHz and 1,800 MHz were auctioned by the Dot in January 2014, and in February of the same year, the winning bidders were awarded the licenses. Following the 2G spectrum scam of 2010, the allocation of the 1,800-MHz spectrum had been cancelled by the Supreme Court, and therefore the government offered 307.2 MHz of 1,800 and 46 MHz of the 900-MHz-wide spectrum for sale. The licenses were valid for 20 years. Vodafone and Bharti had already been using the 900-MHz frequency. They were required to renew their licenses prior to their expiry in November 2014. Reliance Jio was the only company that had all-India 4G license. It was a new entrant into voice service and won the 1800 MHz frequency in 14 circles. The spectrum auction of 2014 generated ₹612 billion (US$ 8.9 billion) revenue for the government. The spectrum auction conducted in 2015 concluded on March 25. It went on for nineteen days and involved 115 rounds of bidding for Spectrum in the 800-MHz, 900-MHz, 1,800-MHz and 2,100-MHz bands. The government accrued a total of ₹109,874 crore (US$16 billion) from the auction. Around 11 per cent of the spectrum available, however, remained unsold. The spectrum auction in 2016 commenced on October 1. Ranging across the seven bands of 700 MHz, 850 MHz, 900 MHz, 1,800 MHz, 2,100 MHz, 2,300 MHz and 2,500 MHz, a total of 2,354.55 MHz of spectrum across twenty-two different circles had been offered for sale. For the first time in India, the 700-MHz band spectrum was offered for allocation through auction. A mere 40 per cent of the spectrum offered for auction got sold, and the reason behind this was suggested again to be the high base price.

Thus, despite being an early adopter of spectrum auctions, it has not quite been a success story for India. Due to problems with the design and rules of the auction, the rolling out of services has been very slow.[12] For example, as noted earlier, in the case of the 1991 auction, many rules came up once the auction was over, e.g., that of restricting the number of licenses that a single operator can possess. Also the decision for the second highest bidder to match the highest bid is something not supported by Auction Theory. From the perspective of Auction Theory, this decision is bound to create disincentive for the bidders and prevent them from bidding truthfully. Also, disclosing policies, which can affect the operators' profits, after the auction (ex post), creates a bad precedent. In such cases, bidders become skeptical about what policies would prevail afterwards, unnecessary speculative activities crop up, leading to untruthful bidding, and the net outcome is an inefficient allocation.

Among the several telecom spectrum license auctions conducted in India so far, the 2010 spectrum auction is regarded as the greatest success story. So the following section provides an elaborate description of this auction.

Radio spectrum auction: 2010

A frequency band through which one can send any electromagnetic signal is known as a spectrum. In many countries like United States, the UK, India etc. governments allocate spectrum licenses to private players. There are several ways in which governments can allocate the rights; auctions, administrative licensing, allocation on a First-Come-First-Served basis and lotteries are some of them. However, in recent times, auction is used predominantly, particularly after the successes of the New Zealand spectrum auction in the 1990s. The government of India, through the Department of Telecommunications, proposed to allot the rights to use certain specified radio spectrum frequencies in the 2.1-GHz band and unpaired in the 2.3-GHz band (the BWA spectrum) through the process of auction in the different telecom service areas in India. Separate auction processes were carried out for allotting 3G spectrum blocks (the 3G Auction) and BWA spectrum blocks (the BWA Auction), respectively.

The auction

The e-auction continued for more than 34 days (from April 9, 2010 to May 19, 2010). It involved 183 rounds of bidding across the areas. Altogether, seventy-one blocks were put up for auction to private players for all the twenty-two service areas in the country. All were sold.

The two dominant objectives commonly associated with an auction are efficiency (social welfare maximisation) and expected revenue maximisation. However, the government of India had specified several objectives in 2010's spectrum license auction, as follows.[13]

Objectives of the auction

- Obtaining a market-determined price of 3G/BWA spectrum through a transparent process
- Ensuring efficient use of the spectrum, avoiding hoarding
- Stimulating competition in the sector
- Promoting rollout of 3G and broadband services
- Maximising revenue proceeds from the auctions
- Resolving congestion issues related to second-generation (2G) mobile services

Auction process and rules

The auction process dictated that each of the auctions was to be a simultaneous ascending e-auction conducted over the Internet. The system was to enable bidders to access the electronic auction system (EAS). For participation in the auctions, this EAS was to be accessed using standard web browsing software. Under the provisions of Section 13(2) of the Information Technology Act 2000, this EAS is a designated computer resource for receiving electronic records.

The Clock Stage was to identify the bidders to be awarded a block in every telecom service area where at least one block is available for auction. This stage required the bidders in each service area to bid for a block that would confer the right to a single spectrum block not linked to any specific frequency. The Clock Stage was to consist of a number of rounds termed the Clock Rounds. These rounds would stop for either of the following cases:

- Once the number of bids at the prices set in the last completed Clock Round falls short of or equals the number of blocks available for each individual service area where spectrum is being auctioned; and
- No opportunities for Bidders to increase their demand in accordance with the Activity Rules remain. The precise conditions under which the Clock Stage can close are subsequently spelt out. The Clock Stage would identify the Winning Bidders in all service areas as well as set a common Winning Price for all blocks within a particular service area.

A Frequency Identification Stage was to follow the Clock Stage. This stage would basically identify specific frequencies for the Winning Bidders. The frequencies thus identified would be simultaneously announced with the outcome of the Clock Stage. The Frequency Identification Stage would be a random identification of frequencies performed automatically by the Electronic Auction System. However, for the purpose of harmonisation of bands and promoting spectrum efficiency, whenever required, the government always reserves the right to change the frequency allocation at any point over the duration of the relevant licenses.

Winning Bidders were required to pay the sum of the relevant winning prices set in the Clock Stage for service areas in which they were allocated a block. As a consequence of the Auction Rules, all winning bidders in a service area in any auction were to have equal winning prices. To leave no room for any doubt, the award of spectrum in any service area was not dependent on the award of spectrum in any other service area. Bidders were not to be allowed to link a bid for spectrum in any service area with the outcome of the auction in any other service areas. This was to say that no bidder was allowed to put in any form of contingent bid.

The GoI allocated one block of 2 × 5 MHz of spectrum in Delhi and Mumbai for MTNL and one block of 2 × 5 MHz of spectrum in the remaining service areas for BSNL. BSNL and MTNL were not supposed to participate in the 3G Auction but rather were required to match the winning price achieved in the respective service areas in the 3G Auction as payment for the spectrum allotted to them.

The GoI allocated one block of 20 MHz of unpaired spectrum in Delhi and Mumbai for MTNL and one block of 20 MHz of unpaired spectrum in the remaining service areas for BSNL. BSNL and MTNL were also not supposed to participate in the BWA Auction but instead were required to match the winning price achieved in the respective service areas in the BWA Auction as payment for the spectrum allotted to them.

The right to use the 3G spectrum was to remain valid for twenty years from the effective date unless revoked or surrendered earlier. However, this could be subject only to the operator continuing to have a UAS/CMTS license. The spectrum usage rights would be treated as withdrawn immediately whenever the UAS/ CMTS license was terminated or cancelled for some reason.

The seven private players who took part in the auction are Vodafone Essar Limited, Tata Teleservices Limited, Bharti Airtel Limited, Reliance Telecom Limited, Aircel Limited, Idea Cellular Limited and S Tel Private Limited. The winning bidders to whom the licenses were to be awarded needed to fulfill some roll-out obligations, which are elaborated next.

Roll-out obligations for 3G spectrum

The licensee to whom the spectrum was assigned would be required to have a network roll-out that reflected the need to provide a reasonable level of service to a wide cross section of customers, as well as ensuring the efficient use of the spectrum.

METRO SERVICE AREA

The licensee to whom the spectrum was assigned would be required to provide the necessary street-level coverage using the 3G spectrum in at least 90 per cent of the service area within five years of the effective date.

CATEGORY A, B AND C SERVICE AREAS

The licensee to whom the spectrum was assigned would be required to ensure that at least 50 per cent of the district headquarters (DHQ) in the service area is covered using the 3G spectrum, out of which at least 15 per cent of the DHQs would have to be rural short-distance charging areas (SDCA), within five years of the effective date.

A licensee who failed to achieve its roll-out obligations was to be allowed a further period of one year to do so by making a payment of 2.5 per cent of the successful bid amount (i.e., spectrum acquisition price) per quarter or part thereof as liquidated damages. If the concerned operator still fails to complete its roll-out obligations even within the extended period of one year, the spectrum assignment would stand as withdrawn.

Roll-out obligations for BWA spectrum

METRO SERVICE AREA

The licensee to whom the spectrum was assigned would be required to provide the required street-level coverage using the BWA spectrum in at least 90 per cent of the service area within five years of the effective date.

CATEGORY A, B AND C SERVICE AREAS

The licensee to whom the spectrum is assigned was required to ensure that at least 50 per cent of the rural SDCAs get covered within five years of the effective date using the BWA spectrum. Coverage of a rural SDCA meant that at least 90 per cent of the area demarcated by the municipal/local body limits should get the required street-level coverage. In the case that the licensee fails to achieve its roll-out obligations, its spectrum assignment would be withdrawn.

Results

The 3G auction resulted in revenue generation worth Rs. 68,263.21 crores to the government of India, the maximum contribution being attributable to Delhi and Mumbai (38.5 per cent of the total revenue). The top five circles together were responsible for 64 per cent of the total revenue. Together, the 3G auction and the BWA auction generated Rs. 106,262 crore, much higher than the expectation of the Indian government (Rs. 35,000 crore). (See Tables 6.1 and 6.2.)

The huge success of the 2010 telecom spectrum auction gave birth to a lot of euphoria and therefore high expectations regarding further auction prospects. Therefore, for the 2G spectrum allocation, the GoI felt auction in a similar manner as conducted during 2010 to be the most appropriate

Table 6.1 Circle-wise the winners and the final bids for the 3G spectrum auction

State/union territory	Reserve price (in Rs. crore)	Price (in Rs. crore)	Successful bidders
Delhi	320	3,316.93	Vodafone, Airtel, Reliance
Mumbai	320	3,247.07	Reliance, Vodafone, Airtel
Karnataka	320	1,579.91	Tata, Aircel, Airtel
Tamil Nadu	320	1,464.94	Airtel, Vodafone, Aircel
Andhra Pradesh	320	1,373.14	Airtel, Idea, Aircel
Maharashtra	320	1,257.82	Vodafone. Tata, Idea
Gujarat	320	1,076.06	Vodafone, Tata, Idea
Kolkata	120	544.26	Vodafone, Aircel, Reliance
Uttar Pradesh (W)	120	514.04	Airtel, Idea, Tata
Uttar Pradesh (E)	120	364.57	Aircel, Idea, Vodafone
Punjab	120	322.01	Idea, Reliance, Tata, Aircel
Rajasthan	120	321.03	Reliance, Airtel, Tata
Kerala	120	312.48	Idea, Tata, Aircel
Madhya Pradesh	120	258.36	Idea, Reliance, Tata
Haryana	120	222.58	Idea, Tata, Vodafone
Bihar	30	203.46	S Tel, Airtel, Reliance, Aircel
West Bengal	120	123.63	Airtel, Reliance, Vodafone, Aircel
Orissa	30	96.98	S Tel, Aircel, Reliance
North East	30	42.3	Aircel, Airtel, Reliance
Assam	30	41.48	Reliance, Airtel, Aircel
Himachal Pradesh	30	37.23	Airtel, S Tel, Idea, Reliance
Jammu and Kashmir	30	30.3	Idea, Aircel, Reliance, Airtel

Source: www.dot.gov.in/spectrum-management/2463 and www.medianama.com/2010/05/223-3g-auction-india-ends-provisional-winners/

Table 6.2 Total amount of bid per player and the number of circles won

Player	Total bid (in Rs crore)	Circle won
Vodafone Essar Limited	11,608.86	9
Tata Teleservices Limited	5,855.29	9
Bharti Airtel Limited	12,295.46	13
Reliance Telecom Limited	8,585.04	13
Aircel Limited	6,499.46	13
Idea Cellular Limited	5,759.59	11
S Tel Private Limited	337.67	3

Source: www.dot.gov.in/spectrum-management/2463 and www.medianama.com/2010/05/223-3g-auction-india-ends-provisional-winners/

allocation mechanism. However, the 2012 spectrum auction failed to repeat the success story of 2010. In the following section, therefore, we present a brief discussion on the 2012 auction just to indicate the contrast between this auction and the 3G auction of 2010.

Radio spectrum auction: 2012

The year 2001 had witnessed the last auction of spectrum in the 2G bands (800-MHz, 900-MHz and 1,800-MHz bands). For the spectrum in these bands, Telecom Regulatory Authority of India (TRAI) never recommended the auction process till August 2007, though in 2006 the auction of spectrum in the 2,100-MHz and 2,300-MHz bands was recommended. The auction of spectrum in the 2G bands was perceived to be infeasible by the TRAI in May 2010. However, in its recommendations in February 2011, TRAI referred to its recommendations of November 2010 about scrapping some licenses issued since 2006 and the consequent availability of spectrum. TRAI reconsidered its earlier decision and recommended the auction of these spectrum licenses to determine the actual price. The Honourable Supreme Court of India, in a judgement dated February 2, 2012 in the writ petitions no 423/2010 and 10/2010, instructed TRAI to make fresh recommendations for allotting license and allocating spectrum in the 2G band in twenty-two service Aaeas through auction in a similar way as had been followed for allocating spectrum in the 3G band, keeping in view the decision taken by the Central Government in 2011. The writ petitions mentioned, "The licences granted to the private respondents on or after 10.1.2008 pursuant to two press releases issued on 10.1.2008 and subsequent allocation of spectrum to the licensees are declared illegal and are quashed."

Following the Honourable Supreme Court's Judgment, the Department of Telecommunication took the following decisions:[14]

- The spectrum would not be bundled with licenses in future.
- Licenses of a "unified license" nature were to be issued to telecom operators, and the license holder could freely choose to offer any of the multifarious telecom services.
- Any license holder interested in offering wireless services would be required to obtain spectrum through a market-determined process.
- No concept of contracted spectrum would be there in future, and thus there would neither be a concept of initial or start-up spectrum.
- Spectrum will be made available only through the market-driven process.
- No more UAS licenses linked with spectrum will be awarded.
- Only unified licenses will prevail in future, and the license should not be linked to the allocation of spectrum anymore.
- Spectrum, if required, will have to be obtained separately.
- The prescribed limit on spectrum assigned to a service provider will be 2×8 MHz/2×5 MHz for GSM/CDMA technologies for all service areas other than in Delhi and Mumbai, where it will be 2×10MHz/ 2×6.25 MHz.

- However, additional spectrum beyond prescribed limits could be acquired by the licensee in the open market, in case an auction of spectrum subject to the limits prescribed for the merger of licences is conducted.
- Spectrum sharing, with respect to spectrum obtained through auction, would be permitted only if the auction conditions provide for it.
- In India, at this stage, no spectrum trading would be allowed.

Spectrum auction

Spectrum assignment has been different for the various spectrum bands for mobile services in India depending upon whether a licensee is deploying CDMA or GSM technology. Therefore, the technology chosen by the licensee gets bound with the spectrum assigned for mobile services. The DoT in 2012 conducted a 2G spectrum auction for both GSM and CDMA bands. Eleven blocks having 1.25 MHz each in the 1,800-MHz frequency band were auctioned, with the exceptions of Mumbai and Delhi, where eight blocks were available. In every circle, three out of eleven blocks were reserved for fresh entrants in the telecom sector or operators whose licenses had been cancelled by the Supreme Court on February 2, 2012, following the 2G spectrum scam. Fresh entrants and companies affected by the Supreme Court judgement were required to win at least four blocks in each circle in order to start or continue their operations in that circle. The incumbent players whose licenses were unaffected by the Supreme Court judgement were allowed to bid for only two blocks in each circle. All circles of Airtel and Vodafone, and some circles for Idea fell in this category.

Initially, three blocks of 1.25-MHz frequency each in the 800-MHz band were available for auction, and the only applicants in the auction for spectrum in the 800-MHz band (CDMA) were Videocon Telecommunications Limited and Tata Teleservices (Tata DoCoMo CDMA). However, both companies withdrew their applications before the last date for withdrawal of applications, which was November 5. On October 29, DoT had announced both Videocon and Tata Teleservices to be pre-qualifiers in the bidding process. Videocon withdrew its application on November 2, quickly followed by the Tata Teleservices. Following these withdrawals, no bidders were left, and the CDMA spectrum auction had to be called off.

The final list of bidders that was announced on November 6 included Bharti Airtel Limited, Idea Cellular Ltd, Telewings Communications Services Private Limited, Videocon Telecommunications Limited and Vodafone South Limited. This was followed by a mock auction on November 7–8 and the e-auction of the 1,800-MHz band began on November 12.

Results

Starting on November 12 and ending on November 14, the auction continued for more than two days and consisted of 14 fourteen rounds. The government received bids worth a total of Rs. 94.07 billion, way below its target of Rs. 280 billion. Not a single bidder submitted a bid for the pan-India spectrum, which had a reserve price of Rs. 140 billion. Bids were tendered on 102 of the 140 blocks being offered. No bid was received for the Delhi, Mumbai, Karnataka and Rajasthan circles. Kapil Sibal, the then minister of communications and information technology, observed on the unsold spectrum, "Of course there will be an auction. There is no doubt about that. What procedure we follow for that auction is something that we will decide in another few weeks."[15] (See Tables 6.3 and 6.4.)

Table 6.3 2G spectrum auction (1,800 MHz)[16]

Service area	Price per block (Rs. crore)	Airtel	Idea	Telewings	Vodafone	Videocon	Total blocks
Andhra Pradesh	286.91			4			4
Assam	8.67	1	4		2		7
Bihar	46.43		1	4	2	4	11
Delhi							0
Gujarat	224.84			4		4	8
Haryana	46.52				2	4	6
Himachal Pradesh	7.78				1		1
Jammu and Kasmir	6.33		4		2		6
Karnataka							0
Kerala	65.3				1		1
Kolkata	113.72		4				4
Madhya Pradesh	53.99				2	4	6
Maharashtra	262.81			4	1		5
Mumbai							0
North East	8.84		4		2		6
Orissa	20.27		4		2		6
Punjab	67.28				1		1
Rajasthan							0
Tamil Nadu	306.09		4				4
Uttar Predesh (East)	76.17			4	1	4	9
Uttar Pradesh (West)	107.41			4	2	4	10
West Bengal	25.84		5		2		7

Source: www.dot.gov.in/spectrum-management/2461

Table 6.4 Total payments made by individual telecommunication operators

Telecommunication operator	Payment (Rs. crore)	Blocks won	Circles
Airtel	8.67	1	1
Idea	2,031.31	30	8
Telewings	4,018.28	24	6
Vodafone	1,127.94	23	14
Videocon	2,221.44	24	6

Source: Calculated from the Table 6.3.

Coal auction

Among the auctions conducted by the Indian government, an important one is the coal auction. Nobody can possibly overlook the importance of coal in contemporary times. Across the world, power generation is an essential component of development. Coal has played a vital role in power generation for almost every country throughout history, which it continues to do in spite of the fact that most governments are making serious efforts to move to the use of renewable energy. Even in recent times, coal accounts for almost 29 per cent of the world's primary power generation. Thus, coal continues to be the principal source of energy. However, the importance of coal is not limited to its being a source of energy. Infrastructure industries, especially the metallurgical sector and steel and cement industry, are largely reliant on coal.

Power generation in India is largely dependent on coal. In fact, India's dependence on coal for power generation is much larger compared to the world standard; coal accounts for 52 per cent of India's primary power and 66 per cent of total power generation. India follows the United States and China to hold the third position internationally in the production of coal resulting from the high demand for power in India. The Indian government in 2003 declared the mission "Power to all by 2012", and since then coal has become even more important for this country.

The government of India has complete control over the exploration for and the extraction of coal in this country. The Ministry of Coal (MOC) among its objectives has the production, supply, distribution and setting and control of the price of coal. The Ministry of Coal is helped in performing these activities from the three government-owned corporations, Coal India Ltd. (CIL), Coal Controller's Organization (CCO) and Central Mine Planning and Design Institute Limited (CMPDIL). The CIL, founded in 1975, has seven coal-producing subsidiaries. It also happens to be the largest coal-producing company in the world. CCO operates directly under MOC and is responsible for various statutory functions such as the collection and publication of statistical information on coal. CMPDIL provides technical support for seven coal-producing subsidiaries in the area of geological exploration and drilling, project planning and designing and so on.

Auction of coal

The Mines and Minerals (Development and Regulation) Act 1957 (MMDR Act 1957) was amended in September 2010, in order to introduce competitive bidding for coal mining rights. Despite the guidelines, the import of both cooking and non-cooking coal recorded a significant increase between 2006 and 2011. Because of this, the CAG conducted an audit titled "Allocation of Coal Blocks and Augmentation of Coal Production" in 2012. This audit report strongly suggested that GOI should finalise the regulations of competitive biddings. The report also suggested that the "auctioning of blocks was considered as one of the widely practiced and acceptable selection process which was transparent and objective". Finally, the report revealed that the delays in introducing the process of competitive bidding have largely benefitted the private companies. This audit has estimated a financial gain of Rs. 1.86 lakh crore that was likely to accrue to private coal block allottees (based on average cost of production and average sale price of opencast mines of CIL in the year 2010–2011). Following this, the central government designed the Auction by Competitive Bidding of Coal Mines Rules 2012. The government also decided by the end of 2014 to auction the coal blocks in mid-February 2015. Subsequently the CIL has been conducting e-auctions on a regular basis at market-driven prices in accordance with the New Coal Distribution Policy (NCDP) provision.

Auction process and rules

As per the Auction Rules, the bidders were required to pay a non-refundable amount of Rs. 5 lakhs in order to be eligible for participation in the auction. The complete process of bid submission would be divided into two stages as follows:

STAGE 1: TECHNICAL BID

In the first stage, bidders would be required to submit:

1 The bid security.
2 The technical bid along with a covering letter.

3   The financial bid to the extent of specifying the initial price offer, which should not be higher than the ceiling price.

The ceiling price for the coal mine is the CIL notified price.

STAGE 2: ELECTRONIC AUCTION – FINAL PRICE OFFER

The initial price offer of the bidders who meet all the eligibility conditions (the "Technically Qualified Bidders") were to be ranked on the basis of the ascending initial price bid submitted by each technically qualified bidder. Based on such a ranking of the technically qualified bidders, holding the first 50 per cent of the ranks (with any fraction rounded off to a higher integer) or five technically qualified bidders, whichever is greater, shall be considered to be qualified for participating in the electronic auction (the "Qualified Bidders").

During the auction process, the qualified bidder would be able to submit its final price offer as many times as it wishes against the same coal mine. The qualified bidder would remain anonymous to the other qualified bidders participating in the electronic auction process, as well as to MSTC/ Nominated Authority. The qualified bidder would be able to see the prevailing lowest final price offer against the coal mine, but the name of the lowest qualified bidder at any point of time will not be displayed. The qualified bidder shall have to put its final price offer below the displayed lowest bid by a decrement of Rs. 2 per tonne to become the lowest qualified bidder. The electronic auction process will have scheduled start and close times, which will be displayed on screen. A qualified bidder will be able to put its final price offer after the start of bid time until the close time of the electronic auction.

As to why the auction was conducted electronically, Coal India[17] listed several benefits of the e-auction process:

* Total transparency in coal marketing
* Equal treatment of all the categories of customers without any discrimination
* Buyers getting coal of their choice with respect to source, grade, size/ mode
* Buyers being able to purchase coal from anywhere in the country
* New consumers, snapped consumers and consumers seeking additional coal over and above their FSA quantity being able to buy coal under this scheme
* Greatly reducing, if not eliminating, the tendency of diverting coal to secondary markets at a premium

- No quota/linkage/sponsorship needed for the purchase of coal
- The option for depositing money for registration/EMD online

Electronic auction (e-auction) for the sale of coal is regularly being conducted at market-driven prices in accordance with the NCDP provision. At present, the CIL is conducting e-auctions under different schemes as follows:[18]

- *Spot e-auction*: Under this scheme, any Indian buyer can procure coal through a consumer-friendly single window in a simple and transparent manner for their own consumption or for trading. Spot e-auction is in operation since November 2007.
- *Special spot e-auction*: Special spot e-auction was introduced during 2015–2016. Any Indian buyer, including traders, can buy coal under a special spot e-auction with a longer validity period of lifting.
- *Special forward e-auction*: The special forward e-auction was introduced in 2015–2016 to make coal available to the power producers with a flexible period of lifting.
- *Exclusive e-auction*: Exclusive e-auction was introduced in 2015–2016 for non-power consumers, including CPP, with a flexible period of lifting.

Results (Table 6.5)

Repo auction

Another auction conducted in India that is worth mentioning is the repo auction conducted by the Reserve Bank of India (RBI). Before going into a detailed description, first let us briefly explain what repo auction means. The *repo auction* is an auction conducted by the central bank of a country (RBI in India) to infuse cash into the banking system. The central bank (RBI) lends money to commercial banks. Commercial banks deposit government and listed corporate bonds as collateral with the central bank (RBI). This also calls for the definition of the *reverse repo auction*, which is an auction conducted by the central bank of a country to remove excess cash from the banking system. Here the central bank issues sovereign bonds to absorb the excess liquidity. Commercial banks can buy these bonds because they will get interest on their excess deposits. The RBI fixes the repurchase rate (repo) in its bimonthly monetary policy review. This is also referred to as the *overnight repo rate*, or the rate at which the RBI is ready to lend money to banks, accepting government securities as collateral.[19]

Banks were previously allowed to borrow up to 0.5 per cent of their net demand and term liabilities (NDTL) through the overnight repo window. A change was brought about in the process in 2014. This was when the RBI decided to move from a fixed repo rate regime to dynamic and variable

Table 6.5 Performance of different e-auction schemes from 2015–2016 to 2017–December 2018

2017–2018 (April–December)

Auction	Spot	Forward	Special forward for power	Exclusive for non-power	Special spot	Total
Total quantity allocated (in mill tonnes)	40.8	Discontinued	27.4	10.7	0.35	79.4
Total notified value (in Rs. crore)	5,705		3,175	1,625	50	10,555
Total booking value (in Rs. crore)	9,453		3,974	2,078	60	15,565
Increase over notified value (in %)	65.7%		25.1%	27.9%	19.5%	47.5%
2016–2017						
Total quantity allocated (in mill tonnes)	53.7	0.29	47	6.3	6.2	113.6
Total notified value (in Rs. crore)	7,421	88	4,949	854	895	14,207
Total booking value (in Rs. crore)	9,288	88	5,734	933	1,075	17,118
% increase over notified value	25.2%	0.8%	15.9%	9.3%	20.1%	20.5%
2015–2016						
Total quantity allocated (in mill tonnes)	57.4	5.9	13.8	1.5		78.6
Total notified value (in Rs. crore)	7,649	705	1,091	163		9,607
Total booking value (in Rs. crore)	10,230	913	1,472	214		12,829
% increase over notified value	33.7%	29.4%	35.0%	31.5%		33.5%

Source: Section 7, Annual Report 2017–18, Ministry of Coal, Government of India, https://coal.nic.in/content/annual-report-2017-18

lending rates. It decided to allow banks to borrow up to 0.75 per cent of NDTL under the RBI's seven- and fourteen-day-term repo window while reducing access to the overnight repo facility to 0.25 per cent of NDTL.[20]

This move enables the RBI to have better control over the rates at more frequent intervals, rather than once every two months i.e., bimonthly. The intention of the RBI is to keep the call money rate close to the repo rate. It also grants the RBI better control over the liquidity situation in the economy.

Considering the liquidity situation in the market, the RBI might want to change the repo rate during the intervening period, thereby injecting money into or pumping money out of the economy. This is where the role of the variable rate repo auction enters the picture.

The RBI conducts variable-rate one-day-term repo auctions every Tuesday and Friday. At this auction, it decides the repo rate and the amount of disbursement available at this window. In this manner, it is able to keep the call money rates closer to the previously decided repo rate.

Currently, it also conducts twenty-eight-day-term repo auctions. As recommended by the Urjit Patel Committee, the RBI would seek to introduce longer-term variable rate repo auctions as well.

Notes

1 This Supreme Court judgement was delivered by Justice P. B. Sawant and Justice S. Mohan on 9.2.1995 in the case between the Union of India and the Cricket Association of Bengal.
2 The discussion on spectrum auctions in India during 1991–2001 is largely based on Chattopadhyay and Chatterjee (2014).
3 Jain (2001),
4 CDMA uses a single spectrum of bandwidth (not slices of bandwidth) for all users in the cell. Each conversation is assigned a unique code. The coded signal is extractable at the receiver, by the use of a complementary code.
5 Babu, P. G. & Das, N. (1999). *Privatization and auctions*. India Development Report.
6 Ibid.
7 3G spectrum auction begins smoothly, top telecom operators in fray. *The Times of India*, April 9, 2010.
8 Official results for 3G Spectrum Auctions: Department of Telecomm – Government of India.
9 *2G Auctions Flop as 57% of Spectrum Remains Unsold; Govt Gets Less Than a Quarter of Its Revenue Target – Economic Times*. Economictimes.indiatimes. com. Retrieved March 3, 2013.
10 https://en.wikipedia.org/wiki/MTS_India
11 PTI 26 Feb 2013, 08.40 pm IST. (2013, February 26). *Spectrum Auction Base Price Too High in India: Vodafone CEO – Economic Times*. Economictimes. indiatimes.com. Retrieved March 2013.
12 Jain, R. S. (2001). Spectrum auctions in India: Lessons from experience. *Telecommunications Policy*, *25*(10–11), 671–688.

13 www.dot.gov.in/sites/default/files/English%20AR%202010-11_1.pdf
14 www.trai.gov.in/sites/default/files/Recommendation_Sepc_Cap_21112017.pdf
15 www.ndtv.com/business/2g-spectrum-auction-flops-fetches-a-meagre-rs-9-407-crore-313279
16 www.dot.gov.in/spectrum-management/2461
17 www.coalindia.in/home/faq.aspx
18 Section 7, Annual Report 2017–18, Ministry of Coal, Government of India, https://coal.nic.in/content/annual-report-2017-18
19 www.quora.com/What-is-variable-rate-repo-auction
20 www.quora.com/What-is-a-repo-auction

7 Other applications of Auction Theory

Introduction

This book has made an attempt to introduce Auction Theory to all including those who are hearing about such a theory for the first time. Chapter 1 has elaborated on auction as an allocation mechanism, along with tracing its historical perspective. How auction has been in use since antiquity for various objects has been discussed in detail in that chapter. Chapter 2 compared and contrasted auction as an allocation mechanism vis-à-vis alternative mechanisms that are used, e.g., First-Come-First-Served, Beauty Contest, grandfathering, Lottery etc. This chapter highlighted the merits of auctions over these mechanisms, thus clearly indicating why auction is growing popular across the world. Chapter 3 laid the theoretical foundations of Auction Theory, explaining how auctions can be analysed as incomplete information games, also elaborating on the different types of auctions and the basis for their classifications. Chapter 4 discussed the major results of Auction Theory under different contexts, the most important one being the famous Revenue Equivalence Principle. This chapter has identified the situations where this principle always works and also the ones where it fails. Chapter 5 narrated various countries' experiences regarding the auction of telecom spectrum licenses. Chapter 6 discussed the telecom spectrum, coal and repo auctions in India.

A tour through the previous chapters of this book makes it clear why Auction Theory needs to be studied at all and how it can help designing auctions in real life. After this tour, the readers are also familiarised with the basic tools and techniques used in Auction Theory. Although in real life, situations are quite different from theoretical constructs, the study of Auction Theory helps in developing the analytical skill that facilitates addressing real-life auction design issues. However, the application of Auction Theory is not limited to the design of auctions alone. The study of Auction Theory can be extended to various other issues as well, e.g., contests and tournaments, search engine design, supply chain management and the like. The real-life auctions discussed the most in the book are the auctions of telecom spectrum licenses. Coal and timber auctions have also been mentioned. But in a multitude of other cases, the use of auction as an allocation mechanism is gaining popularity day by day. One such case is that of tradable emission permits. In this chapter, basically, we aim to elaborate the scope of Auction Theory beyond the design of traditional auctions, thus indicating the applicability of Auction Theory in other disciplines.

Contests and tournaments

Contests and tournaments are the areas where Auction Theory has probably the maximum applicability. Like auctions, contests are also games of incomplete information. Though it may sound strange, contests can be modelled in exactly the same way as auctions. Here the participants, who are also termed the contestants, play analogous roles to the bidders. The ability of each contestant derives from his private information. Thus the abilities constitute the types of the players here. This is quite similar to the valuations of the bidders in auctions, who have private information regarding their maximum willingness to pay. Based on that information, they quote bids, and a payment rule dictates how much they have to pay. In contests, the participants choose what amount of effort to put in on the basis of their private information regarding their abilities. Thus effort as a function of ability can be thought of in identically the same manner as bids are functions of valuations. Here the efforts can be interpreted to be analogous to bids. Just as bids are monotonically increasing functions of valuations, similarly, efforts are also monotonically increasing functions of abilities. This is quite intuitive. If a contestant knows that she possesses high ability, she is more motivated to invest a greater amount of effort. Thus using the same methods that are used to calculate equilibrium bid functions, in the case of contests optimal equilibrium effort functions for contestants can be worked out. If the contest organisers want to extract the best performances from the contestants, they can easily do so by designing the right kind of incentive structure based on the information regarding the effort functions of the contestants. The analysis of tournaments can also be done similarly since tournaments are just one form of contest that involves competition among a relatively large number of contestants. Such contests may involve simultaneous competitions being held at the same venue within a short period of time or a number of matches involving a subset of the total contestants, with the final winner being selected on the basis of the combined result of the individual matches.

Environmental science

The use of auction in implementing environment-related policies is steadily on the rise. As we all know, worldwide pollution control has been a serious concern that is growing day by day. The control of emissions constitutes a substantial part of overall pollution control. One method of controlling emissions has been the traditional method of pollution taxes where a tax or fee is levied on the amount of pollution that a firm or source generates. Due to this tax, profit-maximising firms find it worthwhile to bring down their emission levels to the point where its marginal abatement cost equals the tax rate. However, the main challenge with this taxation system is to identify the appropriate tax rate.[1] This problem is further intensified when the policymakers possess less information regarding the abatement technology and thus the related abatement costs of the firms. The policymakers cannot ex ante be sure of the possible impact of taxation on the incentives of the firms. Due to this problem, a more market-oriented incentive-based approach is preferable, and here enters the role of tradable emission permits. As observed by Stavins (2001):

> *Tradable permits can achieve the same cost-minimizing allocation of the control burden as a charge system, while avoiding the problem of uncertain responses by firms. Under a tradable permit system, an allowable overall level of pollution is established and allocated among firms in the form of permits. Firms that keep their emission levels below their allotted level may sell their surplus permits to other firms or use them to offset excess emissions in other parts of their facilities.*

Tradable emission permits, however, can be allocated in more than one way, e.g., grandfathering, Beauty Contests, Lottery, auctions etc. However, allocation of free pollution permits through such methods may very well act against the objective of reducing emissions, since firms may feel that if they reduce current emissions, they will likely receive fewer permits in future.[2] If any predetermined price is charged for the permits, again the same problem crops up as in the case of taxation: what should the optimal price level be? Since the auction of permits inflicts a cost on the firms, they always have the incentive to reduce their emission levels, as opposed to the case of free allocation of emission permits. At the same time as has been discussed in Chapter 2, auctions always work better in discovering true prices than any other alternative traditional allocation mechanisms. Cramton (2002) observes:

> *An auction of carbon permits is the best way to achieve carbon caps set by international negotiation to limit global climate change. To*

minimize administrative costs, permits would be required at the level of oil refineries, natural gas pipe lines, liquid sellers, and coal processing plants.

Cap-and-trade policy has been quite a success story for alleviating sulphur dioxide emission–related problems in the United States, as elaborated by Stavins, Chan, Stowe and Sweeney (2012).[3] They observe:

The sulphur dioxide (SO₂) allowance-trading programme established under Title IV of the 1990 Clean Air Act Amendments (CAAA) was the world's first large-scale pollutant cap-and-trade system. ("Allowance trading" and "cap-and-trade" are synonymous.) The stated purpose of the Acid Rain Program was to reduce total annual SO_2 emissions in the US by ten million tons relative to 1980, when total US emissions were about 26 million tons. In a departure from conventional environmental regulation, the legislation did not prescribe how power plants would reduce their SO_2 emissions. Instead, with a phase-in beginning in 1995 and culminating in 2000, the statute capped aggregate SO_2 emissions at the nation's 3,200 coal plants and created a market for firms to buy and sell government-issued allowances to emit SO_2. By 2007, annual emissions had declined below the programme's nine million ton goal (a 43% reduction from 1990 levels), despite electricity generation from coal-fired power plants increasing more than 26% from 1990–2007 (EPA 2012; EIA 2011).

Another area where auction is increasingly proving its effectiveness is that of environmental conservation. Palm-Forster et al. (2016) discuss conservation auctions in the context of protecting the aquatic ecosystems in the Great Lakes regions from the agricultural effluents. As Palm-Forster et al. (2016) describe:

In the United States, farmers generally hold the property rights to manage their land as they choose; therefore, most agri-environmental programs are voluntary and many involve payments for ecosystem services (PES) to create incentives to adopt conservation practices However, payments must come from budgets, and budgets are constrained. Spending on federally funded conservation programs is projected to be over $5.5 billion annually during the 5-year life of the 2014 Farm Bill. In order to make best use of these funds, there is growing interest in designing more cost-effective programs in order to generate greater benefits with a limited conservation budget. Researchers and practitioners have called for programs that "pay for performance," which *refers to the desire to pay for environmental outcomes rather than paying for practices or inputs without considering the resulting impact on the environment. In order to obtain the greatest environmental impact from limited funds, two kinds of information are essential: 1) a reliable prediction of environmental benefits from using a best management practice (BMP) on a specific field, and 2) knowledge concerning the least costly incentive that a farmer would be willing to accept in order to adopt that BMP. . . . Research has shown that auctions are more cost-effective when bids are evaluated based on both the cost of BMP implementation and the predicted environmental benefits estimated by appropriate biological simulation models.*

Search engine design and improving the allocation of their sponsored ad slots

In Google and Yahoo, the two most used search engines, we keep encountering various advertisements in different positions and different sequences. The assignment of such positions is also done through auction. As explained by Varian (2007):

Search engine advertising has become a big business, with the combined revenue of industry leaders Yahoo and Google exceeding $11 billion in 2005. Nearly all of these ads are sold via an auction mechanism.

The basic design of the ad auction is fairly simple. An advertiser chooses a set of keywords that are related to the product it wishes to sell. Each advertiser states a bid for each keyword that can be interpreted as the amount that it is willing to pay if a user clicks on its ad.

When a user's search query matches a keyword, a set of ads is displayed. These ads are ranked by bids (or a function of bids) and the ad with the highest bid receives the best position; i.e., the position that is mostly likely to be clicked on by the user. If the user clicks on an ad, the advertiser is charged an amount that depends on the bid of the advertiser below it in the ranking.

Procurement auction

Procurement is a common practice in different types of organisations. For example, academic institutions procure books, computer equipment, laboratory instruments and the like; industrial houses procure different types of machineries. The purchase of such things are quite often done by procurement auctions. These auctions are slightly different from the auctions described in the previous chapters in the sense that here the situation is like a mirror image of the auctions discussed so far. Here the sellers are the bidders, and the buyer is the auctioneer. The buyer may at times delegate the responsibility of conducting auction to some individual or agency that is proficient in designing auctions. Another difference is that here the bids are monotonically decreasing functions of the types. In the auctions, the bidders are asked to quote, in sealed envelopes, prices they will charge for some item(s). After all the quotations are collected, the envelopes are opened and ranked vis-à-vis one another. Then the lowest bidder is chosen to be the winning bidder to whom the right to supply is granted. Here also the equilibrium quotation amounts, which are effectively bids, can be calculated using the tools and techniques of Auction Theory.

At times, procurements involve a slightly more complicated framework. The situation just described involves just quoting prices. However, the suppliers may be asked to quote both the price and the quality of any item. In this case, the bid becomes multidimensional, and to select the winning bidder, some score is used. This score is calculated using a predefined formula. Depending on the rules of the auction, the scores are used to identify the winning bidder(s), and auction formats vary depending on the scoring rules. These sorts of multidimensional auctions are also known as scoring auctions.[4] Scoring auctions are largely used in defense equipment procurements. One ready example is that of the defense auction conducted by the U.S. Department of Defense (DoD), as noted by Che (1993).

In India also, quite often government organisations conduct procurement auctions that involve two components, e.g., the technical bid and the financial bid. The technical bid component is to ensure that all bids come from technically qualified bidders, and the financial bid component identifies the lowest bid among them, and usually the lowest bidder is chosen as the winning bidder.

For "Repair and Renovation of Civil & Electrical Works for 'Copyright Board & Copyright Office CRB&CRO)' at August Kranti Bhawan, Bhikaji Kama Place, New Delhi", bids were invited in May 2014 where the bid document included the technical and the financial bid components.[5] In the case of "Electronic Reverse Auction for Works, Stores and Service Contracts", conducted by the Railway Board under the Ministry of Railways, Government of India, the tender notice issued on March 28, 2018, mentions the requirements of technical and financial bids.[6]

Supply chain management

In the contemporary world, particularly owing to globalisation and digitalisation of trade the role of supply chains is assuming more importance day by day. Chen et.al. (2005) analyse the role of auction in making supply chain procurement more cost-effective and thus efficient. They observe:

> *There is a recent emphasis on using auctions for supply chain procurement (Chin 2003), especially for noncritical components. It has become an effective and efficient means of achieving lower acquisition costs, lower barriers for new suppliers to enter a market, and consequently, better market efficiency. With recent advances in information technology, such auctions can be carried out through the Internet, referred to as online auctions. Online auctions allow geographically diverse buyers and sellers to exchange goods, services, and information, and to dynamically determine prices that reflect the demand and supply at a certain point of time so that efficient matching of supply and demand can be realized. As pointed out by Lucking-Reiley (2000), online auctions often lead to lower information, transaction, and participation costs, as well as increased convenience for both sellers and buyers, the ability for asynchronous bidding, and easier access to larger markets.*

Conclusion

All the above sections are suggestive of the fact that Auction Theory is very effective in addressing a multitude of types of economic problems. Most often auction as an allocation mechanism generates highest level of social efficiency compared to other alternative mechanisms, and that too involving least transaction, information and participation costs. Thus a study of Auction Theory does not just help understanding auctions, but also it develops insights regarding various other issues those are apparently unrelated to auctions. This book has made an attempt to familiarise the readers with theoretical and applied aspects of Auction Theory. As has been stated at the very outset, Auction Theory is a vast area, so only a miniscule portion of it could be covered within the short span of this book. However, we hope that whatever little could be discussed here, will motivate the readers to explore Auction Theory further on their own and also understand its application in dealing with real-life issues along with applying it wherever possible.

Notes

1 Stavins (2001).
2 *Fiscal implications of climate change.* (2008, March). International Monetary Fund, pp. 25–26.

3 https://voxeu.org/article/lessons-climate-policy-us-sulphur-dioxide-cap-and-trade-programme
4 Dastidar (2017) provides a detailed discussion on scoring auctions.
5 http://copyright.gov.in/Documents/Technical%20Bid%20_Volume-I_.pdf
6 www.indianrailways.gov.in/railwayboard/uploads/directorate/Transformation_Cell/Circulars/RB_RA_Letter_dt_28_3_18.pdf

References

Books

Cassady, R. (1967). *Auctions and auctioneering*. Berkeley, CA: University of California Press.

Chatterjee, K., & Samuelson, W. (1983). Bargaining under incomplete information. *Operations research, 31*(5), 835–851.

Che, Y. K. (1993). Design competition through multidimensional auctions. *The RAND Journal of Economics*, 668–680.

Chen, R. R., Roundy, R. O., Zhang, R. Q., & Janakiraman, G. (2005). Efficient auction mechanisms for supply chain procurement. *Management Science, 51*(3), 467–482.

Dastidar, K. G. (2017). *Oligopoly, auctions and market quality*. New York: Springer.

Illing, G., & Klüh, U. (Eds.). (2003). *Spectrum auctions and competition in telecommunications*. Cambridge, MA: MIT Press.

Klemperer, P. (2000). *The economic theory of auctions*. Edward Elgar Publishing.

Klemperer, P. (2004). *Auctions: Theory and practice*. Princeton, NJ: Princeton University Press.

Krishna, V. (2010). *Auction theory*. San Diego, CA: Academic Press.

McMillan, J. (1994). Selling spectrum rights. *Journal of Economic Perspectives, 8*(3), 145–162.

Mas-Colell, A., Whinston Michael, D., & Green Jery, R. (2006). *Microeconomic theory*, Indian Reprint.

Menezes, F. M., & Monteiro, P. K. (2008). *An introduction to auction theory*. Oxford: Oxford University Press.

Milgrom, P. (2004). *Putting auction theory to work*. New York: Cambridge University Press.

Ray, S. (1921). *Ha Ja Ba Ra La*. New Delhi: U. Roy and Sons. (Originally in Bengali, translated to English as *HJBRL: A Nonsense Story* by Jayinee Basu [2005], published by Nishtha, India, ISBN 1-4116-3983-9 [English, translation]).

Palm-Forster, L. H., Swinton, S. M., Redder, T. M., DePinto, J. V., & Boles, C. M. (2016). Using conservation auctions informed by environmental performance models to reduce agricultural nutrient flows into Lake Erie. *Journal of Great Lakes Research, 42*(6), 1357–1371.

Varian, H. R. (2007). Position auctions. *International Journal of Industrial Organization, 25*(6), 1163–1178.

Articles

Babu, P. G., & Das, N. (1999). Privatization and auctions. In *India Development Report*, K. Parikh (ed.). New Delhi: Oxford University Press, 267–278.

Chattopadhyay, S., & Chatterjee, S. (2014). *Telecom spectrum auctions in India: The theory and the practice.* Retrieved from www.iimcal.ac.in/sites/all/files/pdfs/wps_741.pdf

Cramton, P., & Kerr, S. (2002). Tradeable carbon permit auctions: How and why to auction not grandfather. *Energy Policy, 30*(4), 333–345.

Harsanyi, J. C. (1967). Games with incomplete information played by "Bayesian" players, I–III Part I. The basic model. *Management Science, 14*(3), 159–182. Retrieved from www.eyewitnesstohistory.com/slaveauction.htm

Jain, R. S. (2001). Spectrum auctions in India: Lessons from experience. *Telecommunications Policy, 25*(10–11), 671–688. Retrieved from https://economictimes.indiatimes.com/industry/telecom/spectrum-auction-base-price-too-high-in-india-vodafone-ceo/articleshow/18696511.cms

Jilani, A. (2015). Spectrum allocation methods: Studying allocation through auctions. *Journal of Economics, Business and Management, 3*(7), 742–745.

Rose, G. F., & Lloyd, M. (2006, May). *The failure of FCC spectrum auctions (PDF).* Center for American Progress. Retrieved from https://cdn.americanprogress.org/wp-content/uploads/kf/SPECTRUM_AUCTIONS_MAY06.PDF

Sen, A., & Swamy, A. V. (2004). Taxation by auction: Fund raising by 19th century Indian guilds. *Journal of Development Economics, 74*(2), 411–428.

Stavins, R. N. (2001). Economic analysis of global climate change policy: A primer. In *Climate change: Science, strategies, and solutions.* Retrieved from http://citeseerx.ist.psu.edu/viewdoc/download?doi=10.1.1.198.6276&rep=rep1&type=pdf

Stavins, R. N., Chan, G., Stowe, R., & Sweeney, C. (2012). *The US sulphur dioxide cap and trade programme and lessons for climate policy.* Retrieved from https://voxeu.org/article/lessons-climate-policy-us-sulphur-dioxide-cap-and-trade-programme

Van Heck, E., & Ribbers, P. M. (1997). Experiences with electronic auctions in the Dutch flower industry. *Electronic Markets, 7*(4), 29–34.

Van Heck, E., Van Damme, E., Kleijnen, J., & Ribbers, P. (1997, January). New entrants and the role of information technology case-study: The Tele Flower Auction in the Netherlands. In *Proceedings of the thirtieth Hawaii international conference on system sciences* (Vol. 3, pp. 228–237). Wailea, HI: IEEE.

Vickrey, W. (1961). Counterspeculation, auctions, and competitive sealed tenders. *The Journal of Finance, 16*(1), 8–37.

Reports

Fiscal Implications of Climate Change. (2008, March). International Monetary Fund, pp. 25–26. Retrieved April 26, 2010 www.imf.org/external/np/pp/eng/2008/022208.pdf

Official results for 3G spectrum auctions: Department of Telecomm – Government of India.

PTI 26 Feb 2013, 08.40 pm IST. (2013, February 26). Spectrum auction base price too high in India: Vodafone CEO. *Economic Times.* Economictimes.indiatimes. com. Retrieved March 2013, from https://economictimes.indiatimes.com/indus try/telecom/spectrum-auction-base-price-too-high-in-india-vodafone-ceo/article show/18696511.cms

Section 7, Annual Report 2017–18, Ministry of Coal, Government of India. Retrieved from https://coal.nic.in/content/annual-report-2017-18

Tender Notice No. IACS/TC/PC/13/A-08. Retrieved February 11, 2013, from http:// mailweb.iacs.res.in/tender/IACS_TC_PC_13_A-08_11.02.2013.pdf

Thomas, T. P., and Gulveen, A. (2012). 2G auctions flop as 57% of spectrum remains unsold; govt gets less than a quarter of its revenue target. *Economic Times.* Economictimes.indiatimes.com. Retrieved March 6, 2013, from https:// economictimes.indiatimes.com/industry/telecom/2g-auctions-flop-as-57-of-spectrum-remains-unsold-govt-gets-less-than-a-quarter-of-its-revenue-target/ articleshow/17218077.cms

van Damme, E. E. C. (2002). The Dutch UMTS-auction. (CentER Discussion Paper, Vol. 2002–72). Tilburg: Microeconomics. Retrieved from https://pure.uvt.nl/ws/ portalfiles/portal/542759/72.pdf

Weblinks (accessed 06/11/2018)

http://copyright.gov.in/Documents/Technical%20Bid%20_Volume-I_.pdf

https://corporatefinanceinstitute.com/resources/knowledge/deals/ipo-initial-public-offering/

https://corporatefinanceinstitute.com/resources/knowledge/finance/dutch-auction/

https://en.wikipedia.org/wiki/Aalsmeer_Flower_Auction

https://en.wikipedia.org/wiki/Dutch_auction

https://en.wikipedia.org/wiki/MTS_India

www.coalindia.in/home/faq.aspx

www.cramton.umd.edu/papers2000-2004/01nao-cramton-report-on-uk-3g-auction.pdf

www.dot.gov.in/sites/default/files/English%20AR%202010-11_1.pdf

www.dot.gov.in/spectrum-management/2461

www.dot.gov.in/spectrum-management/2463

www.fcc.gov/about-fcc/fcc-initiatives/incentive-auctions

www.indianrailways.gov.in/railwayboard/uploads/directorate/Transformation_Cell/ Circulars/RB_RA_Letter_dt_28_3_18.pdf

www.medianama.com/2010/05/223-3g-auction-india-ends-provisional-winners/

www.ndtv.com/business/2g-spectrum-auction-flops-fetches-a-meagre-rs-9-407-crore-313279

www.paulklemperer.org/PressArticles/FT26Nov2002PDKAuctionsLb.pdf

www.trai.gov.in/sites/default/files/Recommendation_Sepc_Cap_21112017.pdf

www.quora.com/What-is-variable-rate-repo-auction

www.quora.com/What-is-a-repo-auction

Index

For Product Safety Concerns and Information please contact our EU
representative GPSR@taylorandfrancis.com Taylor & Francis Verlag GmbH,
Kaufingerstraße 24, 80331 München, Germany

Printed and bound by CPI Group (UK) Ltd, Croydon, CR0 4YY
08/05/2025
01864535-0001